034527

# How much is enough?

# Other Earthscan/Worldwatch Books

Lester R. Brown et al.

*State of the World 1991*
*State of the World 1992*
*Saving the Planet*

Worldwatch
environmental
alert series
■■■■■■■■■

# How much is enough?

The consumer society and the future of the earth

## Alan Thein Durning

EARTHSCAN
Earthscan Publications Ltd, London

First published in Great Britain 1992
by Earthscan Publications Ltd
120 Pentonville Road, London N1 9JN

"The right of Alan Thein Durning to be identified as the
author of this Work has been asserted in accordance with
the Copyright Designs and Patents Acts 1988"

British Library Cataloguing-in-Publication Data.
A catalogue record for this book is available from the British
Library.

ISBN 1-85383-134-4

Printed and bound by
Biddles Ltd, Guildford and Kings Lynn

Earthscan Publications Ltd is an editorially independent
subsidiary of Kogan Page Ltd and publishes in association
with the International Institute for Environment and
Development and the World Wide Fund for Nature (UK).

# Contents

Acknowledgments                                          7

Foreword                                               11

## I. Assessing Consumption                            17

1. The Conundrum of Consumption                       19
2. The Consumer Society                                26
3. The Dubious Rewards of Consumption                 37
4. The Environmental Costs of Consumption             43

## II. Searching for Sufficiency                   *63*

5. Food and Drink                                  *65*
6. Clean Motion                                    *78*
7. The Stuff of Life                               *89*

## III. Taming Consumerism                         *103*

8. The Myth of Consume or Decline                  *105*
9. The Cultivation of Needs                        *117*
10. A Culture of Permanence                        *136*

For Further Reading and Action                     *151*
Notes                                              *155*
Index                                              *191*

# Acknowledgments

As I write these words in early Spring of 1992 in Washington, D.C., construction crews in Bloomington, Minnesota, are racing to finish the world's largest shopping mall—a monumental agglomeration of retail outlets built around a three-hectare indoor amusement park. Its designers call it "The Mall of America," and if their projections materialize it will attract more visitors each year than Mecca or the Vatican.

The irony of that name has stayed with me over the months I have worked on this book. The Mall of America has become a sort of symbol for my native land. All of the United States seems to be remaking itself in the image of the mall. As a people, I fear, we are now bound together mostly by a commercial culture of sales pitches, national brands, and franchise stores. Shopping centers have become the centers of our public life, and consuming has become both our primary means of self-definition and our leading pastime.

This trend is not uniquely American, of course. Europeans and Japanese are following our lead, jettisoning community as the organizing principle of their lives in favor of private consumption. And the richer citizens of poor nations emulate our consuming ways as best they can. Yet in the perception of most of the world's people, the consumer life-style is made in America, and the Mall of America is all of America.

Bloomington's Mall of America thus stands in my mind as a microcosm—a sort of icon—of what I believe is now the world's prevailing definition of progress: higher consumption. So it is fitting that the Mall of America and this book should reach their completion within months of each other. One displays on an epic scale the consumerist values of the ascendant global culture. The other questions those values on both human and ecological grounds, and argues the necessity of cultivating alternatives. Let the more compelling message prevail!

Although my name alone appears on the cover of this book, many contributed to its creation. Foremost among those I have the privilege to thank is Holly Brough, who worked skillfully and uncomplainingly over the span of almost three years as my associate. She not only gathered and calculated much of the data presented in this volume; she also shaped the book's message with her clear values, joy for life, and finely wrought sense of humor. Whatever merit *How Much Is Enough?*

possesses is as much a tribute to her talents as my own. When, weeks before the book's completion, an opportunity Holly had been hoping for materialized, Vikram Akula took over her responsibilities ably and with great spirit.

The Charles Stewart Mott Foundation of Flint, Michigan, deserves mention next, for trusting enough in this enterprise to support it with a research grant. Few foundations are willing to think so deeply about what our environmental predicament means for our way of life.

Most of Worldwatch Institute's research staff reviewed one draft of this book or another. Those who not only reviewed it but assisted in its research include Nicholas Lenssen, Marcia Lowe, Michael Renner, John Ryan, and John Young. Outside the institute, Herman Daly, Amy Thein Durning, Jean Durning, Manuel Guerra, Petra Kelly, and Edward Wolf all took time from busy schedules to comment on rough-hewn early drafts. For exceptional generosity in sharing information, I thank Ronald Sprout of the U.N. Economic Commission for Latin America and the Caribbean in Washington, D.C., and Vicki Robin of the New Road Map Foundation in Seattle, Washington.

Finally, on a personal note, I would like to thank my grandmother, Elizabeth Cressey, for the example she has provided. Despite the proliferation of wastefulness on all sides, her quiet ethic of conserving has never left her. Through the years she has persisted in taking care of things and giving away much of her modest income. Now 88 years of age, she walks and rides the bus wherever she needs to go (she has never owned an automobile), and, undeterred by failing eyesight, still identifies flowers for those of us who have lived too hurriedly to learn their names. To her I dedicate this book.

Alan Thein Durning

Worldwatch Institute
1776 Massachusetts Ave., N.W.
Washington D.C. 20036

*April 1992*

# Foreword

Consumption: the neglected god in the trinity of issues the world must address if we are to get on a path of development that does not lead to ruin. The other two—population growth and technological change—receive attention, but with consumption there is often only silence.

The silence is not surprising. Breaking it requires the richest one fifth of the globe to question their own lifestyles, to challenge the all-pervasive notion that more is better. For the last 40 years, buying more goods, acquiring more "things," has been the over-riding goal of people in western industrial countries. At the same time, the poorest one fifth of the world has had but one goal: surviving the next day. Finding a bit of food, some wood to burn as fuel, some shelter and clothing for their children. It is now becoming clear that having two fifths of the world—some 2.2 billion people—working toward these very different goals is wreaking havoc on the earth, and that we cannot continue with business as usual.

For those of us in industrial countries, it is also becoming clearer that after a point, more consumption does not equal greater fulfillment. The recent U.S. publication of *The Overworked American*, by Harvard University economist Juliet Schor, struck a chord with many Americans. She points out that since mid-century, when given the choice, we have consistently opted for more money over more time for leisure and family. Yet has this made Americans any happier? Polls indicate the answer is no. We are trapped on a treadmill of more work, more consumer goods, and hence more destruction of the earth.

*How Much Is Enough?* explains the need to break this vicious cycle. Alan Thein Durning argues that the consumer society can only be a passing phase in the world's history—for its own sake and that of the future habitability of the planet. All parents want to give their children a better life, but we must now realize that such a life cannot consist of more cars, more air conditioners, more prepackaged frozen food, more shopping malls. How much better it would be to pass on to our children a world in which their options for meeting everyone's needs for food, education, fulfilling work, shelter, and good health were expanded, not lessened. This will happen only if those of us in the consumer society change our ways.

There are some faint signs that such a change is possible. The consumer splurge of the eighties has given way to an era of lower expectations, albeit in reaction to the recession that gripped many nations. And polls everywhere indicate profound disenchantment with the status quo. Now is the time to channel that frustration into a movement for what Alan calls a culture of permanence—a society that lives within its means; that draws on the interest provided by the earth's resources, not its principal; that seeks fulfillment in a web of friendship, family, and meaningful work. As Alan points out in his final chapter, the linked fates of humanity and the natural realm depend on us, the consumers.

This is the second book in the new Worldwatch Environmental Alert Series, which complements the Institute's other publications—*State of the World*, the Worldwatch Papers, and *World Watch* magazine. In the first, *Saving the Planet*, Lester R. Brown, Christopher Flavin, and Sandra Postel outlined the shape of a sustainable global economy and discussed the instruments of change for achieving that goal. Next in the series is *Last Oasis: Facing Water Scarcity*, by Sandra Postel. Following that, we expect books in the series on renewable energy and population.

We hope that these short, lively books will provide readers with food for thought about why we need to shift to a sustainable path of development—and how to do so.

*Linda Starke, Series Editor*

# How Much Is Enough?

# I

## Assessing
## Consumption

# 1

# The Conundrum
# of Consumption

For Sidney Quarrier of Essex, Connecticut, Earth Day 1990 was Judgment Day—the day of ecological reckoning. While tens of millions of people around the world were marching and celebrating in the streets, Sidney was sitting at his kitchen table with a yellow legal pad and a pocket calculator. The task he set himself was to tally up the burden he and his family had placed on the planet since Earth Day 1970.[1]

Early that spring morning he began tabulating everything that had gone into their house—oil for heating, nuclear-generated electricity, water for showers and watering the lawn, cans of paint, appliances, square footage of carpet, furniture, clothes, food, and thousands of other things—and everything that had come out—garbage pails of junk mail and packaging, newspapers and magazines by the cubic meter, polluted water, and smoke from the furnace. He listed the resources they had tapped to move them around by car and airplane, from fuel and lubricants to tires and replacement parts. "I worked on that list most of the day," Sid remembers. "I dug out wads of old receipts, weighed trash cans and the daily mail, excavated the basement and shed, and used triangulation techniques I hadn't practiced since graduate school to estimate the materials we used in the roofing job."[2]

Manufacturing and delivering each of the objects on his list, Sid knew, had required additional resources he was unable to count. National statistics suggested, for example, that he should double the energy he used in his house and car to allow for what businesses and government used to provide him with goods and services. He visualized a global industrial network of factories making things for him, freighters and trucks transporting them, stores selling them, and office buildings supervising the process. He wondered how much steel and concrete his state needed for the roads, bridges, and parking garages he used. He wondered about resources used by the hospital that cared for him, the air force jets and police cars that protected him, the television stations that entertained him, and the veterinary office that cured his dog.

As his list grew, Sid was haunted by an imaginary mountain of discarded televisions, car parts, and barrels of oil—all piling up toward the sky on his lot. "It was a sober revisiting of that period. . . . It's only when you put together all the years of incremental consumption that you realize the totality." That totality hit him like the ton of paper packaging he had hauled out with the trash over the years: "The question is," Sid said, "Can the earth survive the impact of Sid, and can the Sids of the future change?"[3]

That *is* the question. Sidney Quarrier and his family are no gluttons. "During those years, we lived in a three bedroom house on two-and-a-half acres in the country, about 35 miles from my job in Hartford," Sidney recounts. "But we have never been rich," he insists. "What frightened me was that our consumption was typical of the people here in Connecticut."[4]

Sid's class—the American middle class—is the group that, more than any other, defines and embodies the contemporary international vision of the good life. Yet the way the Quarriers lived for those 20 years is among the world's premier environmental problems, and may be the most difficult to solve.

Only population growth rivals high consumption as a cause of ecological decline, and at least population growth is now viewed as a problem by many governments and citizens of the world. Consumption, in contrast, is almost universally seen as good—indeed, increasing it is the primary goal of national economic policy. The consumption levels exemplified in the two decades Sid Quarrier reviewed are the highest achieved by any civilization in human history. They manifest the full flowering of a new form of human society: the consumer society.

This new manner of living was born in the United States, and the words of an American best capture its spirit. In the age of U.S. affluence that began after World War II, retailing analyst Victor Lebow declared: "Our enormously productive economy . . . demands that we make consumption our way of life, that we convert the buying and use of goods into rituals, that we seek our spiritual satisfaction, our ego satisfaction, in

consumption. . . . We need things consumed, burned
up, worn out, replaced, and discarded at an ever increasing rate." Most citizens of western nations have re-
sponded to Lebow's call, and the rest of the world appears intent on following.[5]

In industrial lands, consumption now permeates social values. Opinion surveys in the world's two largest
economies—Japan and the United States—show that
people increasingly measure success by the amount they
consume. The Japanese speak of the "new three sacred
treasures": color television, air conditioning, and the
automobile. One fourth of Poles deem "Dynasty,"
which portrays the life-style of the richest Americans,
their favorite television program, and villagers in the
heart of Africa follow "Dallas," the television series that
portrays American oil tycoons. In Taiwan, a billboard
demands "Why Aren't You a Millionaire Yet?" A *Business Week* correspondent beams: "The American
Dream is alive and well . . . in Mexico." Indeed, the
words "consumer" and "person" have become virtual
synonyms.[6]

The life-style made in the United States is emulated
by those who can afford it around the world, but many
cannot. The economic fault lines that fracture the globe
defy comprehension. The world has 202 billionaires and
more than 3 million millionaires. It also has 100 million
homeless people who live on roadsides, in garbage
dumps, and under bridges. The value of luxury goods
sales worldwide—high-fashion clothing, top-of-the-line
autos, and the other trappings of wealth—exceeds the
gross national products of two thirds of the world's
countries. Indeed, the world's average income, about
$5,000 a year, is below the U.S. poverty line.[7]

The gaping divide in material consumption between

the fortunate and unfortunate stands out starkly in their impacts on the natural world. The soaring consumption lines that track the rise of the consumer society are, from another perspective, surging indicators of environmental harm. The consumer society's exploitation of resources threatens to exhaust, poison, or unalterably disfigure forests, soils, water, and air. We, its members, are responsible for a disproportionate share of all the global environmental challenges facing humanity, as Chapter 4 documents.

Ironically, high consumption is a mixed blessing in human terms too. People living in the nineties are on average four-and-a-half times richer than their great-grandparents were at the turn of the century, but they are not four-and-a-half times happier. Psychological evidence shows that the relationship between consumption and personal happiness is weak. Worse, two primary sources of human fulfillment—social relations and leisure—appear to have withered or stagnated in the rush to riches. Thus many of us in the consumer society have a sense that our world of plenty is somehow hollow—that, hoodwinked by a consumerist culture, we have been fruitlessly attempting to satisfy with material things what are essentially social, psychological, and spiritual needs.[8]

Of course, the opposite of overconsumption—destitution—is no solution to either environmental or human problems. It is infinitely worse for people and bad for the natural world too. Dispossessed peasants slash-and-burn their way into the rain forests of Latin America, hungry nomads turn their herds out onto fragile African rangeland, reducing it to desert, and small farmers in India and the Philippines cultivate steep slopes, exposing them to the erosive powers of rain. Perhaps half the world's billion-plus absolute poor are caught in a downward spiral of ecological and economic impoverishment. In desperation, they knowingly abuse the land, salvaging the present by savaging the future.[9]

If environmental destruction results when people have either too little or too much, we are left to wonder, How much is enough? What level of consumption can the earth support? When does having more cease to add appreciably to human satisfaction? Is it possible for all the world's people to live comfortably without bringing on the decline of the planet's natural health? Is there a level of living above poverty and subsistence but below the consumer life-style—a level of sufficiency? Could all the world's people have central heating? Refrigerators? Clothes dryers? Automobiles? Air conditioning? Heated swimming pools? Airplanes? Second homes?

Many of these questions cannot be answered definitively, but for each of us in the consumer society, asking is essential nonetheless. Unless we see that more is not always better, our efforts to forestall ecological decline will be overwhelmed by our appetites. Unless we ask, we will likely fail to see the forces around us that stimulate those appetites, such as relentless advertising, proliferating shopping centers, and social pressures to "keep up with the Joneses." We may overlook forces that make consumption more destructive than it need be, such as subsidies to mines, paper mills, and other industries with high environmental impacts. And we may not act on opportunities to improve our lives while consuming less, such as working fewer hours to spend more time with family and friends.

Still, the difficulty of transforming the consumer society into a sustainable one can scarcely be overestimated. We consumers enjoy a life-style that almost everybody else aspires to, and why shouldn't they? Who would just as soon *not* have an automobile, a big house on a big lot, and complete control over indoor temperature throughout the year? The momentum of centuries of economic history and the material cravings of 5.5 billion people lie on the side of increasing consumption.

We may be, therefore, in a conundrum—a problem admitting of no satisfactory solution. Limiting the consumer life-style to those who have already attained it is not politically possible, morally defensible, or ecologically sufficient. And extending that life-style to all would simply hasten the ruin of the biosphere. The global environment cannot support 1.1 billion of us living like American consumers, much less 5.5 billion people, or a future population of at least 8 billion. On the other hand, reducing the consumption levels of the consumer society, and tempering material aspirations elsewhere, though morally acceptable, is a quixotic proposal. It bucks the trend of centuries. Yet it may be the only option.

If the life-supporting ecosystems of the planet are to survive for future generations, the consumer society will have to dramatically curtail its use of resources—partly by shifting to high-quality, low-input durable goods and partly by seeking fulfillment through leisure, human relationships, and other nonmaterial avenues. We in the consumer society will have to live a technologically sophisticated version of the life-style currently practiced lower on the economic ladder. Scientific advances, better laws, restructured industries, new treaties, environmental taxes, grassroots campaigns—all can help us get there. But ultimately, sustaining the environment that sustains humanity will require that we change our values.

# 2

# The Consumer Society

The world has three broad ecological classes: the consumers, the middle income, and the poor. These groups, ideally defined by their per capita consumption of natural resources, emissions of pollution, and disruption of habitats, can be distinguished in practice through two proxy measures: their average annual incomes and their life-styles. (See Table 2-1.)

The world's poor—some 1.1 billion people—includes all households that earn less than $700 a year per family member. They are mostly rural Africans, Indians, and other South Asians. They eat almost exclusively grains, root crops, beans, and other legumes, and they drink mostly unclean water. They live in huts and shanties, they travel by foot, and most of their possessions are constructed of stone, wood, and other substances avail-

TABLE 2-1. *World Consumption Classes, 1992*

| Category of Consumption | Consumers (1.1 billion) | Middle (3.3 billion) | Poor (1.1 billion) |
| --- | --- | --- | --- |
| Diet | meat, packaged food, soft drinks | grain, clean water | insufficient grain, unsafe water |
| Transport | private cars | bicycles buses | walking |
| Materials | throwaways | durables | local biomass |

SOURCE: Worldwatch Institute.

able from the local environment. This poorest fifth of the world's people earns just 2 percent of world income.[1]

The 3.3 billion people in the world's middle-income class earn between $700 and $7,500 per family member and live mostly in Latin America, the Middle East, China, and East Asia. This class also includes the low-income families of the former Soviet bloc and of western industrial nations. With notable exceptions, they eat a diet based on grains and water, and lodge in moderate buildings with electricity for lights, radios, and, increasingly, refrigerators and clothes washers. (In Chinese cities, for example, two thirds of households now have washing machines and one fifth have refrigerators.) They travel by bus, railway, and bicycle, and maintain a modest stock of durable goods. Collectively, they claim 33 percent of world income.[2]

The consumer class—the 1.1 billion members of the global consumer society—includes all households whose income per family member is above $7,500.

Though that threshold puts the lowest ranks of the consumer class scarcely above the U.S. poverty line, they—rather, we—still enjoy a life-style unknown in earlier ages. We dine on meat and processed, packaged foods, and imbibe soft drinks and other beverages from disposable containers. We spend most of our time in climate-controlled buildings equipped with refrigerators, clothes washers and dryers, abundant hot water, dishwashers, microwave ovens, and a plethora of other electric-powered gadgets. We travel in private automobiles and airplanes, and surround ourselves with a profusion of short-lived, throwaway goods. The consumer class takes home 64 percent of world income—32 times as much as the poor.[3]

The consumer class counts among its members most North Americans, West Europeans, Japanese, Australians, and the citizens of Hong Kong, Singapore, and the oil sheikdoms of the Middle East. Perhaps half the people of Eastern Europe and the Commonwealth of Independent States are in the consumer class, as are about one fifth of the people in Latin America, South Africa, and the newly industrializing countries of Asia, such as South Korea.[4]

For most of us in the consumer society, the proposition that our way of life is exceptionally affluent no doubt seems farfetched. After all, we live modestly compared with the truly rich, and making ends meet is often a struggle. Just as the world's top fifth—the consumer class—makes the remainder appear impoverished, the top fifth of the consumer class—the rich—makes the lowly consumers seem deprived. In the United States, for example, the highest paid fifth of income-earners takes home more than the remaining four fifths combined, and top corporate executives earn 93 times as much as the factory workers they employ. The relation between the rich and the consumer class is a microcosm of that between the consumer class and all people. The rich earn more, consume more natural resources, and disturb ecological systems more than average consumers do. Still, on a global scale, the rich are best taken as a subset of the consumer class, because, in terms of ecological impacts, the greatest disparities are not between the rich and the consumers but between the consumers and the middle-income class.[5]

The emergence of the consumer society is evident in the skyrocketing consumption that has become the hallmark of our era. Worldwide, since mid-century the per capita consumption of copper, energy, meat, steel, and timber has approximately doubled; per capita car ownership and cement consumption have quadrupled; plastic use per person has quintupled; per capita aluminum consumption has grown sevenfold; and air travel per person has multiplied 33 times. Surging consumption of these things—each associated with disproportionate environmental damage—is mostly a reflection of the fortunes of the consumer class. Consumption in the middle-income class has grown more slowly, and among the poor, consumption has remained virtually unchanged.[6]

The consumer society was born in the United States in the twenties, when brand names became household words, when packaged, processed foods made their widespread debut, and when the automobile assumed its place at the center of American culture. Economists and business executives, concerned that the output of mass production might go unsold when people's natural desires for food, clothing, and shelter were satisfied, began pushing mass consumption as the key to continued economic expansion. The "democratization of consumption" became the unspoken goal of American economic policy. Consumption was even painted as a patriotic duty. A business group called the National Prosperity Bureau distributed posters of Uncle Sam exhorting, "Buy what you need now!"[7]

The Great Depression and World War II stalled the democratization of consumption temporarily, but shortly after the war's end, mass consumption came of age. In 1946, *Fortune* magazine heralded the arrival of a "dream era . . . The Great American Boom is on." By 1950, young American families were moving into 4,000 new houses each day, and filling those houses with baby carriages, clothes dryers, dishwashers, refrigerators, washing machines, and—especially—televisions. A year later, the U.S. Bureau of Labor Statistics acknowledged the rising tide of consumerism by adding televisions, electric toasters, frozen foods, canned baby foods, and do-it-yourself perm lotions to the articles tallied in its cost of living index.[8]

In 1953, the chairman of President Eisenhower's Council of Economic Advisers canonized the new economic gospel: The American economy's "ultimate purpose," he proclaimed, was "to produce more consumer goods." Subsequent generations have faithfully pursued that aim. On average, people in the United States today own twice as many automobiles, drive two-and-a-half times as far, use 21 times as much plastic, and cover 25 times as much distance by air as their parents did in 1950.[9]

Since its birth in the United States, the consumer society has moved far beyond American borders, yet its most visible symbols remain American. The Disneyland near Tokyo attracts almost as many visitors each year as Mecca or the Vatican. Coca-Cola products are distributed in over 170 countries. Each day, a new Mc-Donald's restaurant opens somewhere in the world. Singaporean youngsters can brush their teeth with the Teenage Mutant Ninja Turtle Talking Toothbrush, which says "Hey, Dudes!" in Malay. The techniques of mass marketing first perfected in the United States are now employed on every continent, teaching former East Germans, for example, to "Taste the West. Marlboro."[10]

The consumer society's core had already expanded from the United States to Western Europe and Japan by the sixties. Taken together, France, West Germany, and the United Kingdom have almost doubled their per capita use of steel, more than doubled their intake of cement and aluminum, and tripled their paper consumption since mid-century, with the most rapid growth in the fifties and sixties. Per capita consumption of heavily packaged and processed frozen foods doubled in Europe in the eighties, and in the latter half of that decade, soft-drink consumption—mostly in disposable containers—jumped by 30 percent per person. Automobiles, too, multiplied in Europe in the eighties, surpassing households in number in 1988.[11]

Japan started further behind the United States than Europe did in consumption, but rapidly closed the gap. Per person, the Japanese of today consume more than four times as much aluminum, almost five times as much energy, and 25 times as much steel as people in Japan did in 1950, with most of the growth occurring before the energy crises of the seventies. They also own four times as many cars per capita and, just since 1975, eat nearly twice as much meat apiece. They are flying more as well: In 1972, 1 million Japanese traveled abroad; in 1990, the number topped 11 million. Today, after four decades of consumerist expansion, West European and Japanese consumption levels are only one notch below those in the United States.[12]

Across North America, Western Europe, and Japan, home appliances have become standard accoutrements of life. In all three regions, virtually every home has a refrigerator and a washing machine. Clothes dryers and dishwashers are spreading swiftly, and in the United States, air conditioning—which relies on ozone-depleting coolants—was standard in two thirds of homes by 1987, using 13 percent of U.S. electricity. Likewise, nearly 60 percent of Japanese homes now have at least a single-room air conditioner. Microwave ovens and video cassette recorders found their way into nearly two thirds of U.S. homes during the eighties alone. (See Figure 2-1.)[13]

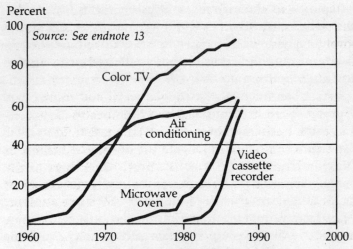

FIGURE 2-1. *U.S. Household Ownership of Appliances, 1960-88*

The eighties were a decade of marked extravagance in all these core regions of the global consumer society. Laissez-faire economic policies and newly internationalized stock and bond markets created an easy-money euphoria among the well to do, which translated into a "get it while you can" binge in the middle echelons of the consumer society. In the United States, not since the Roaring Twenties had conspicuous consumption been so lauded. Over the decade, personal debt matched national debt in soaring to new heights, as consumers filled their houses and garages with third cars, motor boats, home entertainment centers, and whirlpool baths. Between 1978 and 1987, sales of Jaguar automobiles increased eightfold, and the average age of first-time buyers of fur coats fell from 50 to 26. To protect their possessions, Americans spent more on private security guards and burglar alarms than they paid through taxes for public police forces.[14]

Japan also experienced a consumerist binge during the eighties. By decade's end the government was urging loyal Japanese to buy more, hoping to reduce the nation's massive and internationally resented trade surplus by inflating domestic consumption. A wave of stratospheric spending—gold-wrapped sushi and mink coats for dogs—resulted, but Japan still comes to high consumption hesitantly. Many older Japanese hold to their time-honored belief in frugality. Yorimoto Katsumi of Waseda University in Tokyo writes, "Members of the older generation . . . are careful to save every scrap of paper and bit of string for future use." Says one student, "Japanese people are materialistically well-off, but not inside. . . . We never have time to find ourselves, or what we should seek in life."[15]

Far outpacing growth of the consumer class itself is

the spread of consumerism, a cultural orientation that holds that, as British economist Paul Ekins writes, "the possession and use of an increasing number and variety of goods and services is the principal cultural aspiration and the surest perceived route to personal happiness, social status and national success." Since 1953, for example, the Institute of Statistical Mathematics has asked Japanese citizens to select the philosophy that most closely approximates their own. The share selecting "live a pure and just life" fell from 29 percent in the first survey to 9 percent in the mid-eighties, while the share opting to "live a life that suits your own taste" rose from 21 to 38 percent.[16]

Galloping consumerism shows up even more strikingly in surveys from the United States. Between 1967 and 1990, the share of Americans entering college who believed it essential to be "very well off financially" rose from 44 to 74 percent. The share who believed it essential to develop a meaningful philosophy of life dropped from 83 to 43 percent. A student at Cornell University in Ithaca, New York, summed up his peers' aspirations when he told *American Demographics* magazine, "My parents are happy with their life-styles. It's not enough for me."[17]

Similarly, high school seniors polled from 1976 to 1990 displayed waning interest in "finding purpose and meaning in life," and expanding appetites for the artifacts of the consumer society. The percentage ranking "having lots of money" as "extremely important" rose from less than half in 1977 to almost two thirds in 1986, making it first on the list of life goals. More detailed survey questions confirmed consumerism's hold. Desires jumped dramatically for second cars, recreational vehicles, vacation homes, appliances, up-to-date fashions, and late-model automobiles.[18]

The consumer class's membership includes perhaps half the citizens of the formerly socialist states of Eastern and Central Europe, and if those nations succeed in hitching their economies to the world market, they may bring most of their people into its ranks within a decade or two. A young man in a Budapest bar captured his country's consuming mood when he told a western reporter: "People in the West think that we in Hungary don't know how they live. Well, we do know how they live, and we want to live like that too." Says German banker Ulrich Ramm, "The East Germans want cars, videos and Marlboros." Seventy percent of those living in the former East Germany hope to enter the world's automobile class soon; they bought 1 million used western cars in 1991 alone.[19]

Consumerist attitudes are also increasingly evident at the margins of the world economy, where not even elites are members of the consumer class. On the arid Deccan plateau of central India, tribal villagers who never before practiced the tradition of dowry prevalent among upper-caste Hindus are now demanding consumer goods from prospective spouses as the price of an arranged marriage.[20]

More broadly, the emergence of an Indian middle class with about 100 million members, along with liberalization of the market and the introduction of buying on credit, has led to explosive growth in sales of everything from automobiles and televisions to frozen dinners. The streets of Indian cities are now choked with some of the world's most dangerous traffic and worst air pollution, thanks to millions of motor scooters and cars flooding onto routes formerly populated mostly by bicycles, buses, and ox carts. With 14 million televisions in

Indian homes, delivering commercial messages in India's dozens of languages, the *Wall Street Journal* gloats, "The traditional conservative Indian who believes in modesty and savings is gradually giving way to a new generation that thinks as freely as it spends."[21]

*Fortune* magazine is similarly excited about rapidly industrializing nations. In South Korea, it predicts: "More, of everything. More housing, and thus more telephones, appliances, TV sets, furniture, light bulbs, and toilets and toilet cleaners." In Indonesia, reports the *Far Eastern Economic Review*, "construction crews work day and night to erect vast shopping malls, air conditioned marble labyrinths where almost any local or imported luxury can be purchased—at a price." Advertising, which sows the seeds of consumerism, is one of the nation's fastest-growing industries. Mexico is also abuzz with consumerist ambitions: car sales jumped by a quarter in the first half of 1991, and shopping malls and fast food outlets are sweeping the country.[22]

The wildfire spread of the consumer life-style around the world marks the most rapid and fundamental change in day-to-day existence the human species has ever experienced. Over a few short generations, we have become car drivers, television watchers, mall shoppers, and throwaway buyers. The tragic irony of this momentous transition is that the historic rise of the consumer society has been quite effective in harming the environment, but not in providing people with a fulfilling life.

# 3

# The Dubious Rewards
# of Consumption

"The avarice of mankind is insatiable," wrote Aristotle 23 centuries ago, describing the way that as each desire is satisfied, a new one seems to appear in its place. That observation forms the first precept of economic theory, and is confirmed by much of human experience. A century before Christ, the Roman philosopher Lucretius wrote: "We have lost our taste for acorns. So [too] we have abandoned those couches littered with herbage and heaped with leaves. So the wearing of wild beasts' skins has gone out of fashion. . . . Skins yesterday, purple and gold today—such are the baubles that embitter human life with resentment."[1]

Nearly 2,000 years later, Leo Tolstoy echoed Lucretius: "Seek among men, from beggar to millionaire, one who is contented with his lot, and you will not find

one such in a thousand. . . . Today we must buy an
overcoat and galoshes, tomorrow, a watch and a chain;
the next day we must install ourselves in an apartment
with a sofa and a bronze lamp; then we must have car-
pets and velvet gowns; then a house, horses and carriages, paintings and decorations."²

Contemporary chroniclers of wealth concur. For
decades Lewis Lapham, born into an oil fortune, has
been asking people how much money they would need
to be happy. "No matter what their income," he reports, "a depressing number of Americans believe that if
only they had twice as much, they would inherit the
estate of happiness promised them in the Declaration of
Independence. The man who receives $15,000 a year is
sure that he could relieve his sorrow if he had only $30,-
000 a year; the man with $1 million a year knows that all
would be well if he had $2 million a year. . . . Nobody,"
he concludes, "ever has enough."³

If human desires are in fact infinitely expandable,
consumption is ultimately incapable of providing fulfillment—a logical consequence ignored by economic
theory. Indeed, social scientists have found striking evidence that high-consumption societies, just as high-liv-
ing individuals, consume ever more without achieving
satisfaction. The allure of the consumer society is powerful, even irresistible, but it is shallow nonetheless.

Measured in constant dollars, the world's people have
consumed as many goods and services since 1950 as all
previous generations put together. Since 1940, Americans alone have used up as large a share of the earth's
mineral resources as did everyone before them combined. Yet this historical epoch of titanic consumption
appears to have failed to make the consumer class any
happier. Regular surveys by the National Opinion Re-

search Center of the University of Chicago reveal, for
example, that no more Americans report they are "very
happy" now than in 1957. The "very happy" share of
the population has fluctuated around one third since the
mid-fifties, despite near-doublings in both gross national product and personal consumption expenditures
per capita.[4]

A landmark study in 1974 revealed that Nigerians,
Filipinos, Panamanians, Yugoslavians, Japanese, Israe-
lis, and West Germans all ranked themselves near the
middle on a happiness scale. Confounding any attempt
to correlate material prosperity with happiness, low-income Cubans and affluent Americans both reported
themselves considerably happier than the norm, and citizens of India and the Dominican Republic, less so. As
psychologist Michael Argyle writes, "There is very little
difference in the levels of reported happiness found in
rich and very poor countries."[5]

Any relationship that does exist between income and
happiness is relative rather than absolute. The happiness that people derive from consumption is based on
whether they consume more than their neighbors and
more than they did in the past. Thus, psychological data
from diverse societies such as the United States, the
United Kingdom, Israel, Brazil, and India show that the
top income strata tend to be slightly happier than the
middle strata, and the bottom group tends to be least
happy. The upper classes in any society are more satisfied with their lives than the lower classes are, but they
are no more satisfied than the upper classes of much
poorer countries—nor than the upper classes were in the
less affluent past. Consumption is thus a treadmill, with
everyone judging their status by who is ahead and who is
behind.[6]

That treadmill yields some absurd results. During the casino years of the mid-eighties, for example, many New York investment bankers who earned "only" $600,000 a year felt poor, suffering anxiety and self-doubt. On less than $600,000, they simply were unable to keep up with the Joneses. One despondent dealmaker lamented, "I'm nothing. You understand that, nothing. I earn $250,000 a year, but it's nothing, and I'm nobody."[7]

From afar, such sentiments appear to reflect unadulterated greed. But on closer inspection they look more like evidence of humans' social nature. We are beings who need to belong. In the consumer society, that need to be valued and respected by others is acted out through consumption. As one Wall Street banker put it to the *New York Times*, "Net worth equals self-worth." Buying things becomes both a proof of self-esteem ("I'm worth it," chants one shampoo advertisement) and a means to social acceptance—a token of what turn-of-the-century economist Thorstein Veblen termed "pecuniary decency." Much consumption is motivated by this desire for approval: wearing the right clothes, driving the right car, and living in the right quarters are all simply ways of saying, "I'm OK. I'm in the group."[8]

In much the same way that the satisfaction of consumption derives from matching or outdoing others, it also comes from outdoing last year. Thus individual happiness is more a function of rising consumption than of high consumption as such. The reason, argues Stanford University economist Tibor Scitovsky, is that consumption is addictive: each luxury quickly becomes a necessity, and a new luxury must be found. This is as true for the young Chinese factory worker exchanging a radio for a black-and-white television as it is for the German junior executive trading in a BMW for a Mercedes.[9]

Luxuries become necessities between generations as well. People measure their current material comforts against the benchmark set in their own childhood. So each generation needs more than the previous did to be satisfied. Over a few generations, this process can redefine prosperity as poverty. The ghettos of the United States and Europe have things such as televisions that would have awed the richest neighborhoods of centuries past, but that does not diminish the scorn the consumer class heaps on slum dwellers, nor the bitterness felt by the modernized poor.[10]

With consumption standards perpetually rising, society is literally insatiable. The definition of a "decent" standard of living—the necessities of life for a member in good standing in the consumer society—endlessly shifts upward. The child whose parents have not purchased the latest video game feels ashamed to invite friends home. Teenagers without an automobile do not feel equal to their peers. In the clipped formulation of economists, "Needs are socially defined, and escalate with the rate of economic progress."[11]

The relationships between consumption and satisfaction are thus subtle, involving comparisons over time and with social norms. Yet studies on happiness indicate a far less subtle fact as well. The main determinants of happiness in life are not related to consumption at all—prominent among them are satisfaction with family life, especially marriage, followed by satisfaction with work, leisure to develop talents, and friendships.[12]

These factors are all an order of magnitude more significant than income in determining happiness, with the ironic result that, for example, suddenly striking it rich can make people miserable. Million-dollar lottery winners commonly become isolated from their social networks, lose the structure and meaning that work for-

merly gave their lives, and find themselves estranged
from even close friends and family. Similarly, analysts
such as Scitovsky believe that reported happiness is
higher at higher incomes largely because the skilled jobs
of the well-off are more interesting than the routine
labor of the working class. Managers, directors, engineers, consultants, and the rest of the professional elite
enjoy more challenging and creative pursuits, and therefore receive more psychological rewards, than those
lower on the business hierarchy.[13]

Oxford University psychologist Michael Argyle's
comprehensive work *The Psychology of Happiness* concludes: "The conditions of life which really make a difference to happiness are those covered by three
sources—social relations, work and leisure. And the es-
tablishment of a satisfying state of affairs in these
spheres does not depend much on wealth, either absolute or relative." Indeed, some evidence suggests that
social relations, especially in households and communities, are neglected in the consumer society; leisure likewise fares worse among the consumer class than many
assume.[14]

The fraying social fabric of the consumer society,
though it cannot be measured, reveals itself poignantly
in discussions with the elderly. In 1978, researcher
Jeremy Seabrook interviewed scores of older people in
the English working class about their experience of rising prosperity. Despite dramatic gains in consumption
and material comforts their parents and grandparents
could never have hoped for, they were more disillu-
sioned than content. One man told Seabrook, "People
aren't satisfied, only they don't seem to know why
they're not. The only chance of satisfaction we can
imagine is getting more of what we've got now. But it's

what we've got now that makes everybody dissatisfied. So what will more of it do, make us more satisfied, or more dissatisfied?"[15]

The elders Seabrook interviewed were afraid for their children, who they saw as adrift in a profoundly materialistic world. They were afraid of vandals, muggers, and rapists, who seemed ruthless in a way they could not understand. They felt isolated from their neighbors, and unconnected to their communities. Affluence, as they saw it, had broken the bonds of mutual assistance that adversity once forged. In the end, they were waiting out their days in their sitting rooms, each with his or her own television.[16]

Mutual dependence for day-to-day sustenance—a basic characteristic of life for those who have not achieved the consumer class—bonds people as proximity never can. Yet those bonds have severed with the sweeping advance of the commercial mass market into realms once dominated by family members and local enterprise. Members of the consumer class enjoy a degree of personal independence unprecedented in human history, yet hand in hand comes a decline in our attachments to each other. Informal visits between neighbors and friends, family conversation, and time spent at family meals have all diminished in the United States since mid-century.[17]

Indeed, the present generation of young Americans believes that being good parents is equivalent to providing lots of goodies. Raising a family remains an important life goal for them, but spending time with their children does not. According to the survey research of Eileen Crimmins and her colleagues at the University of California, Los Angeles, American high school seniors express a strong desire "to give their children better op-

portunities than they have had," but not to "spend more
time with their children." In high schoolers' minds,
"better opportunities" apparently means "more
goods." Writing in *Population and Development Review*,
the researchers note, "Who would have foreseen a decade ago that clothes with designer labels and computer
video games would be 'essential' inputs to a happy
child?"[18]

Over the past century, the mass market has taken over
an increasing number of the productive tasks once provided within the household, diminishing people's practical reliance on one another. More and more, flush with
cash but pressed for time, we opt for the conveniences of
prepared, packaged foods, miracle cleaning products,
and disposable everythings—from napkins to cameras.

Part of the reason for this transformation of the
household economy is that as consumer-class women
emancipated themselves from the most tedious types of
housework, men did not step in to fill the gap. Instead,
housework shifted into the mass market, paid for out of
the proceeds of women's new jobs. As both men and
women left the home, gutting the household economy,
housework was shunted to the money economy.

The sexual imbalance in housework persists, and, if
anything, women's total workload has grown as the
household changed from a unit of joint production and
consumption into a passive, consuming entity. American women in the early sixties, for example, did as many
hours of housework as their grandmothers had done in
the twenties, despite dozens of "labor-saving" devices.
And while American women, on average, have reduced
their hours of housework somewhat since 1965, most of
them have also taken jobs outside the home. American
men's hours of housework, meanwhile, have barely in-

creased at all since 1965. Data from the United Kingdom suggest a similar trend there.[19]

The commercialization of the household economy has cost the natural world dearly. Chores that shift out of the house take more resources to perform. Shirts pressed in commercial establishments require two trips, often by car, to the laundry. Meals from the take-out restaurant or the frozen foods section multiply the packaging materials and transport energy used to nourish a family.

In the ideal household in the consumer society, people do little for themselves. We do not cook our food from scratch (55 percent of America's consumer food budget is spent on restaurant meals and ready-to-eat convenience foods). We neither mend nor press nor make our own clothes. We neither bake nor build nor do repairs for ourselves. We produce little besides children, and once we have done that, we have a diminishing role. Day-care franchises are more expedient for watching youngsters than the old-fashioned, now dispersed, extended family. Disposable diapers (typically 3,000 of them in the first year, at a cost of $570) have displaced cloth ones.[20]

The evolution of the household from producer to consumer is evident in housing designs in affluent nations. Older houses had pantries, workshops, sewing rooms, built-in clothes hampers, and laundry chutes. New homes have compact kitchens equipped for little more than heating prepared foods. Laundry rooms and root cellars gave way to hot tubs and home entertainment centers. Basement workshops were compressed into utility closets, to make room for pool tables and large-screen televisions. Even gardening, one of the vestigial forms of household production still popular among the consumer class, is gradually turning into a form of consumption, as purchased inputs replace backyard resources. Britons, for example, spent about $3 billion on their gardens and lawns in 1991, up from $1 billion a decade earlier.[21]

Like the household, the community economy has atrophied—or been dismembered—under the blind force of the money economy. Shopping malls, superhighways, and "strips" have replaced corner stores, local restaurants, and neighborhood theaters—the things that help create a sense of common identity and community in an area. Traditional communities are all but extinct in some nations. In the United States, where the demise of local economies is furthest advanced, many neighborhoods are little more than a place to sleep, where neighbors share only a video rental franchise and a convenience store. Americans move, on average, every five years, and develop little attachment to those who live near them.[22]

The transformation of retailing is a leading cause of the decline of traditional community in the global consumer society. (See Chapter 9.) British researchers Carl Gardner and Julie Shepard describe the way civic and collective identity erode with the dwindling of local merchants. "The town center, once the natural focus for the people who live and work there, has . . . lost its individual characteristics and any reference to its unique past. Now it is merely a cloned version of dozens of others up and down the country. Outside shopping hours . . . many town and city centers have, as a result of the retail mono-culture, become shuttered, barren, lifeless spaces."[23]

Another human cost of the consumer society appears to be an acceleration of the pace of life. Psychologist

Robert Levine of California State University, Fresno, measured everything from the average walking speed on city streets to the average talking speed of postal clerks in six countries to show that the pace of life accelerates as countries industrialize and commercialize. Japanese urbanites moved fastest, followed by Americans, English, Taiwanese, and Italians. Indonesians moved most slowly of all. As nations get richer, in other words, they hurry up.[24]

Renegade economist E.F. Schumacher proposed an economic law canonizing that observation in 1978: "The amount of genuine leisure available in a society is generally in inverse proportion to the amount of labor-saving machinery it employs." The more people value time—and therefore take pains to save it—the less able they are to relax and enjoy it. Leisure time becomes too valuable to "waste" in idleness, and even physical exercise becomes a form of consumption. In 1989, Americans devoted the wages of 1 billion working hours to buying such sports clothing as Day-Glo Lycra body suits, wind-tunnel-tested bicycling shoes, rain jackets woven from space-age polymers, and designer hiking shorts. Leisure wear has replaced leisure as the reward for labor. In Japan, meanwhile, a *reja bumu* (leisure boom) has combined with rising concern for nature to pump up sales of fuel-guzzling four-wheel-drive Range Rovers from England and cabins made of imported American logs.[25]

Working hours in industrial countries, despite the reductions trade unionists have won in the past century, still exceed typical working hours before the Industrial Revolution. "In medieval Europe," observes Witold Rybczynski, a professor of architecture at McGill University in Montreal who studies leisure, "religious festivals reduced the work year to well below the modern level of 2,000 hours."[26]

The consumer society fails to deliver on its promise of fulfillment through material comforts because human wants are insatiable, human needs are socially defined, and the real sources of personal happiness are elsewhere. Indeed, the strength of social relations and the quality of leisure—both crucial psychological determinants of happiness in life—appear as much diminished as enhanced in the consumer class. The consumer society, it seems, has impoverished us by raising our income.

# 4

# The Environmental Costs
# of Consumption

Economists use the word consume to mean "utilize economic goods," but the *Shorter Oxford Dictionary*'s definition is more appropriate to ecologists: "To make away with or destroy; to waste or squander; to use up." The economies that cater to the global consumer society are responsible for the lion's share of the damage that humans have inflicted on common global resources.[1]

The consumer class's use of fossil fuels, for example, causes an estimated two thirds of the emissions of carbon dioxide from this source. (Carbon dioxide is the principal greenhouse gas.) The poor typically are responsible for the release of a tenth of a ton of carbon apiece each year through burning fossil fuels; the middle-income class, half a ton; and the consumers, 3.5 tons. In the extreme case, the richest tenth of Americans pump 11 tons into the atmosphere annually.[2]

Parallel class-by-class evidence for other ecological hazards is hard to come by, but comparing industrial countries, home to most of the consumers, with developing countries, home to most of the middle-income and poor, gives a sense of the orders of magnitude. Industrial countries, with one fourth of the globe's people, consume 40-86 percent of the earth's various natural resources. (See Table 4-1.)[3]

From the crust of the earth, we take minerals; from the forests, timber; from the farms, grain and meat; from the oceans, fish; and from the rivers, lakes, and aquifers,

TABLE 4-1. *Consumption of Selected Goods, Industrial and Developing Countries, Late Eighties*

| Good | Industrial Countries' Share of World Consumption | Consumption Gap Between Industrial and Developing Countries |
|------|--------------------------------------------------|-------------------------------------------------------------|
|      | (percent) | (ratio of per capita consumption rates) |
| Aluminum | 86 | 19 |
| Chemicals | 86 | 18 |
| Paper | 81 | 14 |
| Iron and steel | 80 | 13 |
| Timber | 76 | 10 |
| Energy | 75 | 10 |
| Meat | 61 | 6 |
| Fertilizers | 60 | 5 |
| Cement | 52 | 3 |
| Fish | 49 | 3 |
| Grain | 48 | 3 |
| Fresh water | 42 | 3 |

SOURCE: See endnote 3.

fresh water. The average resident of an industrial country consumes 3 times as much fresh water, 10 times as much energy, and 19 times as much aluminum as someone in a developing country. The ecological impacts of our consumption even reach into the local environments of the poor. Our appetite for wood and minerals, for example, motivates the road builders who open tropical rain forests to poor settlers, resulting in the slash-and-burn forest clearing that is condemning countless species to extinction.

High consumption translates into huge impacts. In industrial countries, the fuels burned release perhaps three fourths of the sulfur and nitrogen oxides that cause acid rain. Industrial countries' factories generate most of the world's hazardous chemical wastes. Their military facilities have built more than 99 percent of the world's nuclear warheads. Their atomic power plants have generated more than 96 percent of the world's radioactive waste. And their air conditioners, aerosol sprays, and factories release almost 90 percent of the chlorofluorocarbons that destroy the earth's protective ozone layer.[4]

As people climb from the middle-income to the consumer class, their impact on the environment makes a quantum leap—not so much because they consume more of the same things but because they consume different things. For example, South African blacks, most of them in the middle-income class, spend their limited budgets largely on basic food and clothing, things that are produced with relatively little damage to the environment. Meanwhile, South Africa's consumer-class whites spend most of their larger budgets on housing, electricity, fuel, and transportation—all more damaging to the environment.[5]

Jyoti Parikh and his colleagues at the Indira Gandhi

Institute for Development Research in Bombay used
U.N. data to compare consumption patterns in more
than 100 countries. Ranking them by gross national
product per person, they noticed that as income rises,
consumption of ecologically less damaging products
such as grains rises slowly. In contrast, purchases of
cars, gasoline, iron, steel, coal, and electricity, all ecologically more damaging to produce, multiply rapidly.[6]

The furnishings of our consumer life-style—things
like automobiles, throwaway goods and packaging, a
high-fat diet, and air conditioning—can only be provided at great environmental cost. Our way of life depends on enormous and continuous inputs of the very
commodities that are most damaging to the earth to produce: energy, chemicals, metals, and paper. In the
United States, those four industries are all in the top five
of separate industry-by-industry rankings for energy intensity and toxic emissions, and similarly dominate the
most-wanted lists for polluting the air with sulfur and
nitrogen oxides, particulates, and volatile organic compounds.[7]

In particular, the fossil fuels that power the consumer
society are its most ruinous input. Wresting coal, oil,
and natural gas from the earth permanently disrupts
countless habitats; burning them causes an overwhelming share of the world's air pollution; and refining them
generates huge quantities of toxic wastes. Estimating
from the rough measure of national averages, the consumer class depends on energy supplies equal to at least
2,000 kilograms per capita of average-grade coal a year.
The poor use energy equal to less than 400 kilograms
per person, and the middle-income class falls in between. (See Table 4-2.)[8]

Fortunately, once people join the consumer class,

TABLE 4-2. *Per Capita Consumption of Energy, Selected Countries, 1989*

| Country | Energy |
|---|---|
| | (kilograms of coal equivalent) |
| United States | 10,127 |
| Soviet Union | 6,546 |
| West Germany | 5,377 |
| Japan | 4,032 |
| Mexico | 1,689 |
| Turkey | 958 |
| China | 810 |
| Brazil | 798 |
| India | 307 |
| Indonesia | 274 |
| Nigeria | 192 |
| Bangladesh | 69 |

SOURCE: See endnote 8.

their impact ceases to grow as quickly because their attention tends to switch to high-value, low-resource goods and services. Eric Larson of Princeton University studies the use of chemicals, energy, metals, and paper in both industrial and developing countries. He has found that per capita consumption of most of these things has been stable in industrial countries since the mid-seventies, after surging upward in preceding decades.[9]

Larson attributes some of the change to higher energy prices, but argues that a more fundamental transition lies behind it. In the places that best exemplify the global consumer society, he believes, markets for bulky products such as automobiles and appliances and for infrastructure-building raw materials such as cement are largely saturated. We consumers are spending our extra earnings on high-tech goods and services, from computers and compact disk players to health insurance and fitness club memberships, all of which are gentler to the environment than were earlier generations of consumer goods.[10]

That per capita resource use in the consumer class reaches a plateau is a hopeful sign, yet the plateau is far too high for all the world's people to attain without devastating the planet. Already, the natural systems that sustain our societies are fraying badly, demonstrating that our global economy is getting too big for the global biosphere. If all the world's people were responsible for carbon dioxide concentrations on a par with the consumer class, global emissions of this greenhouse gas would multiply threefold. If everyone in the world used as much metal, lumber, and paper as we consumers do, mining and logging—rather than tapering off as ecological health necessitates—would jump more than threefold.[11]

The influence of the consumer class is felt strongly in regions populated mostly by the middle-income and poor classes. By drawing on resources far and near, we consumers cast an ecological shadow over wide regions of the earth. Every piece of merchandise in the retail districts of the consumer society creates its own ecological wake. A blouse in a Japanese boutique may come from Indonesian oil wells by way of petrochemical plants and textile mills in Singapore, and assembly industries in Bangladesh. Likewise, an automobile in a German showroom that bears the logo of an American-owned corporation typically contains parts manufactured in a dozen or more countries, and raw materials that originated in a dozen others.[12]

A strawberry in a Chicago supermarket in February is likely to have come from Mexico, where it might have been grown with the help of pesticides made in the Rhine Valley of Germany and a tractor made in Japan. The tractor, perhaps constructed with Korean steel cast from iron ingots dug from the territory of tribal peoples in Papua New Guinea, was likely fueled with diesel pumped from the earth in southern Mexico. At harvest time, the strawberry may have been packed in a box made of cardboard from Canadian softwood pulp, wrapped in plastic manufactured in New Jersey, and loaded on a truck made in Italy with German, Japanese, and American parts. The ecological wakes of the blouse, car, and strawberry—like the production lines themselves—span the globe.

Sadly, hard-pressed developing nations sell their ecological souls all too often in the attempt to make ends meet. Cynically playing one nation against another, manufacturing industries have segmented their production lines into dozens of countries in search of low wages, cheap resources, and lax regulations. The Philippine government, more blatant than most, ran an advertisement in *Fortune* in 1975 for the little-regulated Baatan export processing zone: "To attract companies . . . like yours . . . we have felled mountains, razed jungles, filled swamps, moved rivers, relocated towns . . . all to make it easier for you and your business to do business here."[13]

Brazil provides a vivid illustration of what transpires at the tail end of these global production lines. Burdened with an international debt exceeding $100 billion, the government has subsidized and promoted export industries. As a result, the nation has become a major exporter of aluminum, copper, gold, steel, appliances, beef, chicken, soybeans, and shoes. The consumer class gets cheaper products because Brazil is in the export business, but Brazil—most of whose citizens are middle-income—gets stuck with the tab of pollution, land degradation, and forest destruction. As of 1988, for example, 18 percent of the electricity used by all Brazilian industries went to plants producing aluminum and steel for export to industrial countries. Most of that electricity came from gargantuan hydroelectric dams that flooded tropical forests and displaced native peoples from their ancestral domain.[14]

The global consumer society casts a particularly long shadow over forests and soils. El Salvador and Costa Rica, for example, grow export crops such as bananas, coffee, and sugar on more than one fifth of their cropland. Export cattle ranches in Latin America and southern Africa have replaced rain forest and wildlife range. At the consumer end of the production line, Japan imports 70 percent of its corn, wheat, and barley, 95 percent of its soybeans, and more than 50 percent of its wood, much of it from the rapidly vanishing rain forests of Borneo.[15]

The Netherlands imports the agricultural output of three times as much land in developing countries as it has within its borders. Many of those agricultural imports flow to the nation's mammoth factory farms. There, millions of pigs and cows are fattened on palm-kernel cake from deforested lands in Malaysia, cassava from deforested regions of Thailand, and soybeans from pesticide-doused expanses in the south of Brazil in order to provide European consumers with their high-fat diet of meat and milk.[16]

In 1989, the European Community, Japan, and North America between them imported $136 billion worth of "primary commodities"—crops and natural resources—in excess of what they exported. Developing regions, meanwhile, are net exporters of these goods; in the few cases in which they import a particular commodity, much of it goes to their own world-class consumers. About three fourths of developing-country imports of grains—excluding rice—feed livestock, the meat of which largely goes to urban elites.[17]

For decades, shifting tastes among the consumer class have fueled commodity booms in the tropics. Sugar, tea, coffee, rubber, palm, coconut, ivory, gold, silver, gems—each has transformed natural environments and shaped the lives of legions of workers. Today, the tastes of the consumer class retain that influence, as the wildlife trade and illegal drug production illustrate.

Each year, smugglers take millions of tropical birds, fish, plants, animal pelts, and other novelties from impoverished to wealthy lands. They take Olive Ridley and hawksbill sea turtle shells by the thousands, and pelts of jaguars and other spotted cats by the ton. Although habitat destruction is the world's leading cause of species extinction, biologists believe that more than a third of the vertebrates on the endangered species list are there primarily because of hunting for trade. That hunting is fueled by the demand of affluent consumers. Worldwide, sales of exotic wildlife exceed $5 billion a year, according to the World Wildlife Fund in Washington, D.C.[18]

High prices and fast-changing fashions can swiftly drive species to the brink of survival. Peruvian butterflies sell for as much as $3,000 on the black market, and to some Asian consumers, the allegedly aphrodisiac musk from Himalayan deer is worth four times its weight in gold. Bangladesh, India, and Indonesia send

250 million Asian bullfrogs each year to Europe, where restaurants serve their legs as a delicacy. Back in Asia, the mosquitos that frogs eat have proliferated, increasing deaths from malaria, which mosquitos carry.[19]

Another token of consumer-class influence is scrolled out across 200,000 hectares of what used to be the untouched cloud forest of the Peruvian Amazon. The area, once home to a unique highland ecosystem roamed by jaguars and spectacled bears, now boasts the herbicide-poisoned heartland of the world's cocaine industry. In the upper Huallaga Valley, peasants fleeing from poverty in their mountain villages grow coca to feed the cocaine habit of urbanites in the United States and Europe. Coca growers, like farmers of any high-value export crop, spare no expense in its cultivation, plowing up steep slopes and lacing the soil with chemical herbicides to maximize harvests.[20]

Processing the coca leaves compounds the ecological ruin. In 1987, Peruvian forester Marc Dourojeanni estimated that secret cocaine laboratories in the jungle spilled millions of gallons of kerosene, sulphuric acid, acetone, and toluene into the valley's watershed. And the valley's streams have since proved deadly to many types of fish, amphibians, and reptiles. Finally, the rule of drug traffickers and allied guerrilla movements has created a lawless state in which profiteering gangs log, hunt, and fish the region to its destruction.[21]

Thus from global warming to species extinction, we consumers bear a huge burden of responsibility for the ills of the earth. Yet our consumption too seldom receives the attention of those concerned about the fate of the planet, who focus on other contributors to environmental decline. Consumption is the neglected variable in the global environmental equation. In simplified terms, an economy's total burden on the ecological systems that undergird it is a function of three variables: the size of the population, average consumption, and the broad set of technologies—everything from dinner plates to communications satellites—the economy uses to provide goods and services. Generally, environmentalists work on regulating and changing technologies, and family planning advocates concentrate on slowing population growth.

There are good reasons for emphasizing technology and population. Technologies are easier to replace than cultural attitudes. Family planning has enormous human and social benefits aside from its environmental pluses. Yet the magnitude of global ecological challenges requires progress on all three fronts. Environmental economist Herman Daly of the World Bank points out, for example, that simply stopping the growth in rates of global pollution, ecological degradation, and habitat destruction—not reducing those rates, as is clearly necessary—would require within four decades a twentyfold improvement in the environmental performance of current technology. And that assumes both that industrial countries immediately halt the growth of their per-capita resource consumption, allowing the developing countries to begin catching up, and that world population no more than doubles in that period.[22]

Changing technologies and methods in agriculture, transportation, urban planning, energy, and the like could radically reduce the environmental damage caused by current systems, but a twentyfold advance is farfetched. Autos that go three or four times as far on a tank of fuel are feasible; ones that go 20 times as far would defy the laws of thermodynamics. Bicycles, buses, and trains are the only vehicles that can reduce the environmental costs of traveling that much, and to most in the consumer class they represent a lower standard of living. Clothes dryers, too, might run on half as much energy as the most efficient current models, but the only way to dry clothes with one twentieth the energy is to use a clothesline—another retrogressive step, in the eyes of the consumer society.

So technological change and population stabilization cannot suffice to save the planet without their complement in the reduction of material wants. José Goldemberg of the University of São Paulo and an international team of researchers conducted a careful study of the potential to cut fossil fuel consumption through maximizing efficiency and making full use of renewable energy. The entire world population, they concluded, could live at roughly the level of West Europeans in the mid-seventies—with things like modest but comfortable homes, refrigeration for food, clothes washers, a moderate amount of hot water, and ready access to public transit, augmented by limited auto use.[23]

The study's implicit conclusion, however, is that the entire world could not live in the style of Americans, with their larger homes, more numerous electrical gadgets, and auto-centered transportation. Goldemberg's scenario, furthermore, may be too generous. It would not reduce global carbon emissions by anything like the 60–80 percent that the Intergovernmental Panel on Climate Change believes necessary to stabilize the world's climate.[24]

Even assuming rapid progress in stabilizing human numbers and great strides in employing clean and efficient technologies, human wants will overrun the biosphere unless they shift from material to nonmaterial ends. The ability of the earth to support billions of human beings depends on whether we continue to equate consumption with fulfillment.

Some guidance is thus needed on what combination of technical changes and value changes would make a comfortable—if nonconsumer—life-style possible for all without endangering the biosphere. From a purely ecological perspective, the crucial categories are energy, materials, and ecosystems, but such categories are abstract. For a more tangible approach, the next section focuses on three aspects of daily life: what we eat and drink (Chapter 5), how we get around (Chapter 6), and the things we buy and use (Chapter 7). In each case, the world's people are distributed unevenly over a vast range, with those at the bottom consuming too little for their own good—and those at the top consuming too much for the earth's good.

# II

# Searching for Sufficiency

# 5

# Food
# and Drink

The global food consumption ladder has three rungs. At both the bottom and the top, human health and the environment suffer. The question is, Can the world's people converge in the middle while still spreading some of the advantages of the top to all?

The world's poorest billion people are unable to provide themselves with an adequate diet; perhaps half of them are so short of calories that they are likely to suffer stunted growth, mental retardation, or even death. They subsist on grains, especially rice and corn, and root crops such as cassava and potatoes, and they drink water that is often contaminated with human, animal, and chemical wastes. If hunger doesn't kill them, the water may: waterborne diseases account for 80 percent of illness in the Third World, according to the World Health Organization.[1]

Most of the hungry poor are subsistence farmers or landless laborers in less-fertile regions of Africa and Asia, and their hand-to-mouth struggle for survival often comes at the expense of the environment. They trigger soil erosion by cultivating steep or arid land best left for grazing. They denude tree cover while gathering fodder for their animals and wood for their cookfires. The hungry billion clearly have too little.[2]

On the next rung, the 3.3 billion people of the world's middle-income class (those earning $700-7,500 per family member) get plenty of calories and protein from their grain and vegetable diet, giving them healthy basic nourishment. Because they cannot afford to buy much meat, poultry, or dairy products, they eat a low-fat diet, commonly receiving less than 20 percent of their calories from fat and thereby protecting themselves from the diseases associated with excessive dietary fat. They take more than 80 percent of their liquid refreshment in the form of clean drinking water, with the remainder coming from beverages such as tea, coffee, beer, and, for children, milk.[3]

What is absent from this diet is the diversity of fruits and vegetables that would ensure people get all essential nutrients. They also suffer more food poisoning and intestinal parasites than people in the consumer class because they lack safe ways to store their provisions—airtight containers and refrigeration, for example. Their food consumption has environmental consequences, of course. The flooded rice paddies of China are among the many sources of the greenhouse gas methane that is accumulating in the atmosphere, and countless corn fields in Mexico are losing topsoil down great gullies. Yet the middle-income class gets its food at less cost to the earth than either the hungry poor or the consumer class. Its members can afford to leave ecologically fragile arid and forestlands alone, yet they cannot afford a rich diet transported long distances in throwaway wrappers.[4]

The top of the global food ladder is populated by those in the consumer class, who dine on meat, processed and packaged foods, and beverages in disposable containers. Our diet has the nutritional benefits of diversity—we can eat what we wish any time of year—and a fresh, sanitary food supply. But we are victims of our own success: our diet is too rich in fats. Consumers dine on more than a kilogram of meat each week, and we therefore obtain close to 40 percent of our calories from fat. (See Table 5-1.) Most authorities on nutrition now recommend that fats provide no more than 30 percent

TABLE 5-1. *Meat Consumption Per Capita, Selected Countries, 1990*

| Country | Meat[1] |
|---------|---------|
|         | (kilograms) |
| United States | 112 |
| France | 91 |
| Argentina | 82 |
| Soviet Union | 70 |
| Brazil | 47 |
| Japan | 41 |
| Mexico | 40 |
| China | 24 |
| Turkey | 16 |
| Philippines | 16 |
| Egypt | 14 |
| India | 2 |

[1]Beef, veal, pork, lamb, mutton, goat, and poultry in carcass weight equivalents. Poultry figures are for 1989.

SOURCE: See endnote 5.

of calories, and recent research suggests levels below 20 percent are most healthful. The price the consumer class pays for its meat-rich diet is high death rates from the so-called diseases of affluence—heart disease, stroke, and cancer of the breast and colon.[5]

The earth pays for the consumer class's high-fat diet too. As is true of the poor and middle-income classes, grain is the foundation of the consumer class diet. But consumers do not eat the grain itself; we feed it to animals and then eat the animals' meat, milk, and eggs. That conversion process is inefficient because the animals only turn some of the grain into these edible products. In the United States, for example, producing each kilogram of beef served requires 5 kilograms of corn and soybean meal. As a consequence, feeding the meat-eating class takes nearly 40 percent of the world's grain, grown on close to one fourth of the world's cropland.[6]

By using such a large share of the world's grain harvest, the consumer class makes itself disproportionately responsible for the environmental ills associated with that production: eroded soils, depleted aquifers, and streams polluted with fertilizers and pesticides. In the United States, producing each kilogram of beef uses more than 3,000 liters of water—mostly to irrigate feed—and the equivalent of 2 liters of gasoline to produce fertilizer and other farm inputs.[7]

Fortunately, health concerns are already shifting the consumer class's attention from red meat to poultry. Americans, for example, now eat more poultry than beef—an ecological plus because chickens require 40 percent less feedgrain for each unit of meat. In the long run, sustaining the environment will require sharp cuts in meat consumption. The consumer class may have to trim half or more of the grain-fed animal products from its diet to bring itself in line with the earth's resources.[8]

Hope that such a future is possible comes from the growing popular support for the dozens of organizations across the industrial world that are working to restrain the excesses of meat production. Health advocates such as Public Voice on Food and Health Policy in Washington, D.C., argue for rewriting government nutrition guidelines and farm policies that boost meat consumption. Reforming farm policies is especially important since in both the United States and Europe, animal and feed farmers currently receive more than half of all agricultural subsidies. Environmental groups such as the Natural Resources Defense Council, meanwhile, are targeting federal subsidies to grazing on public lands in the western United States. And animal rights groups such as California-based Earthsave and the Vegetarian Society of the U.K. are educating the consumer class about the ecological benefits of eating less meat.[9]

Other environmental costs of the consumers' diet arise less from what we eat than from what happens to it before we get it. In the consumer society, food and beverage processing, packaging, distribution, and storage are all done in ways that tax the earth. In the United States, to take an illustrative case, the consumer food chain in its entirety uses about 17 percent of all energy: 3 percent for livestock production, 3 percent for other types of agriculture, 6 percent for food processing and packaging, and 5 percent to transport, sell, refrigerate, and cook the food and to wash the dishes afterwards.[10]

Adequate processing and packaging protects food from spoiling and contamination. But in the consumer class—the junk food class—much is excessive, amplifying the ecological burden of nourishing people. Frozen foods commonly require 10 times more energy to produce than their fresh counterparts. Unfortunately, the trend in the consumer class is toward replacing fresh with frozen, driven, no doubt, by men's failure to undertake additional housework when women go to work outside the home. In 1960, 92 percent of the potatoes Americans ate were fresh; in 1989, Americans ate almost as many frozen potatoes, mostly french fries, as fresh ones. Per person sales of ready-made frozen meals doubled in Western Europe in the eighties, while in Japan, shoppers stocked their refrigerators with 300 tons of chilled or frozen pizza each week in 1987.[11]

Packaging food for the consumer class absorbs mountains of metal, glass, paper, cardboard, and plastic. One fourth of the aluminum—the most energy-intensive of metals to produce—used in the United States makes cans, and almost half of them are dumped in landfills. Indeed, the United States throws away more aluminum in the form of cans than all but seven other nations use for all purposes. In Japan, beverage cans are the fastest-growing use of aluminum, and half of corrugated cartons package processed foods. Food packaging accounts for a fifth of municipal solid waste in the United States when measured by weight—130 kilograms per person per year in the late eighties—and a substantially larger share when measured by volume.[12]

Much packaging is purely cosmetic. Tomatoes and green peppers that last a week are sold in foam and plastic trays that last a century. And the trend is toward more packaged foods, not fewer. To give just one illustration, according to a *Packaging* magazine survey, 27 percent of older Americans living alone used single-serving packaged foods at least three times a week in 1991, up from 18 percent a year earlier.[13]

The soaring consumption of packaged fare around

the world is perhaps most visible in the beverage industry. At a growing rate, the consumer class drinks beer, soda, bottled water, and other prepared commercial beverages packaged in single-use containers. Ironically, where tap water is purest and most accessible, its use as a beverage is declining. It now typically accounts for only a quarter of drinks in industrial countries. In the extreme case of the United States, per capita consumption of soft drinks rose to 182 liters in 1990 (nearly seven times the global mean), compared with water intake of 141 liters. Americans, in other words, now drink more soda pop than water from the kitchen faucet.[14]

Soft drinks are taking the world by storm. International consumption rose from 64 billion 12-ounce servings in 1980 to an estimated 85 billion in 1990. Much of this growth was driven by the fierce rivalry of two firms, PepsiCo. Ltd. and the Coca-Cola Company, that between them sell their products in virtually every country on earth. Coca-Cola, in particular, is such a global company that it earns 80 percent of its operating income outside the United States. *Adweek*, a trade journal, was so impressed with the brand's success that it praised Coke's mastery of global marketing with a two-page spread depicting Hitler, Lenin, Napoleon, and a Coke bottle. "Only one," ran the caption, "launched a campaign that conquered the world." And the company sees boundless markets for its products. Says Coca-Cola president Donald R. Keough, "When I think of Indonesia—a country on the Equator with 180 million people, a median age of 18, and a Moslem ban on alcohol—I feel I know what heaven looks like."[15]

Such global marketing would cause no ecological offense if soft drink containers were refilled instead of thrown away. No beverages are especially dangerous to nature in themselves. What matters is the way they are packaged. The small amount of beer and soft drinks the world's poor and middle-income classes buy is almost always in refillable bottles, and the other things they drink, such as tea, are packaged minimally, transported in dry form, and prepared on the spot.[16]

The consumer class, in contrast, quenches its thirst increasingly from throwaway containers. The world makes and tosses away at least 200 billion bottles, cans, plastic cartons, and paper and plastic cups each year. Single-handedly, Tetra Pak—the largest manufacturer of multilayer paper-foil-and-plastic drink boxes—made 54 billion cartons worldwide in 1989. Throwaways are all but universal in North America and much of Europe, and they are gaining rapidly in Japan, climbing from 30 percent of commercial beverages in 1980 to 70 percent of a much larger total in 1987. Japanese consumers are even drinking more of their tea and coffee from heated cans: some 80 cans apiece in 1990.[17]

The consumer class might gladly be rid of much food packaging. In many places, fed-up individuals are already expressing their discontent. The Women's Environment Network in the United Kingdom recently organized a "Wrapping Is a Rip Off" campaign, urging members to tear excess packaging from food as they filled their shopping carts. Clearly, the benefits of packaging are available with a fraction as much materials use. In Nicaragua, for example, as in much of the Third World, families who want juice from the corner store bring along a pitcher to carry it in.[18]

Refillable beverage bottles are staging a comeback in Europe, where environmentalists have scored some stunning victories in recent years. More than a decade ago, groups in Denmark defined the ultimate in packaging-free consumption, winning a national ban on throwaway beer and soft drink containers. Virtually every drink container in the country is refilled. Finland, Germany, the Netherlands, and Norway are all moving aggressively to promote reuse and recycling of food and beverage packaging. And activists in most places where the consumer class lives are spreading the philosophy that, for containers, once is not enough. In New Zealand, for example, three major environmental groups have started a "Save Our Bottles" campaign to continue the nation's use of refillable glass milk bottles—which carried nearly all the nation's milk until the recent introduction of throwaway plastic jugs.[19]

The affluent diet also rings up an ecological bill through its heavy dependence on long-distance transport. Over the past century, as diversified small farms gave way to single-crop megafarms and as the price of hauling freight fell relative to consumers' income, food has moved ever longer distances to market. California now supplies more than 40 percent of U.S. fresh produce—at a high energy cost. It takes three times as much energy to truck a head of lettuce from California to New York as it does to grow it. The typical mouthful of American food travels 2,000 kilometers from farm field to dinner plate.[20]

Even the water Americans drink is moving longer distances. Soaring bottled-water consumption involves moving by truck—the least energy-efficient mode of freight transport—water that is often no purer than what comes from the tap. Some of that water is even shipped across oceans: in 1989, Americans bought 190 million liters of imported water. (One of the great ironies of the eighties, dubbed the Safe Water and Sanitation Decade by the United Nations, was the extraordinary commer-

cial success enjoyed by Perrier, which shipped its product to members of the consumer class around the world
while international aid programs to provide safe drinking water to more than a billion people failed for lack of
funding.)[21]

Food retailing, too, has changed in ways that lengthen
the distance food travels. The concentration of shopping of all types in larger stores has increased driving.
Whereas 2 percent of all kilometers that Americans
drove in 1969 were on shopping trips, including food
shopping, by 1983 the figure was 13 percent. The neighborhood green grocers, bakeries, and butcher shops that
still predominate in much of the world disappeared
years ago in the United States. Now the supermarkets
that replaced them are giving way to so-called hypermarkets. In the eighties, the number of supermarkets
declined by one tenth, the average floor space expanded
by half, and the average number of goods in stock doubled to 30,000. Convenience stores specializing in packaged, processed fare, meanwhile, rushed in to fill the
widening spaces between the new hypermarkets; their
number has grown by half since 1980. The net effect of
food retailing polarizing into distant hypermarkets and
intermittent convenience stores is to increase both driving and junk food consumption.[22]

The supply lines that feed the consumer class encircle
the globe. From large urban supermarkets, they fan out
to Philippine plantations, American grain fields, African
rangeland, and Indian spice farms. North Europeans eat
lettuce trucked from Greece. Japanese dine on Australian ostrich meat by the ton and American cherries by
the airplane-load. One fourth of the grapes Americans
eat come from 7,000 kilometers away, in Chile, and half
the orange juice they drink comes from Brazil. Euro-

peans get fruit from as far away as Australia and New Zealand. Even the flowers that decorate the tables of the consumer class come from afar: European winter supplies are flown in from farms in Kenya, while American winter supplies are flown from Colombia.[23]

These global supply lines leave indelible marks on the terrestrial ecosystems they traverse. Malaysian planters spray lindane and aldrin—chemicals forbidden in the United States—on the cocoa that turns into sweets for the consumer class. Cattle ranching for export to American, European, and Middle Eastern consumers is one motive behind the clearing of millions of hectares of South and Central American rain forests, while commercial ranches in Botswana that produce beef for Europe have decimated the nation's herds of migrating wildebeests.[24]

Coastal ecosystems are affected as well. Banana plantations on Saint Lucia in the Caribbean have taken over much of the island's tropical forestland and driven small farmers into the hills, where their slash-and-burn crop cultivation allows soil to wash downstream, choking coastal seagrass ecosystems with silt. Sugar plantations in Fiji that supply the European Community have taken over 4,000 hectares of mangrove forest—despite the low agricultural yields of converted mangrove soils. (Mangroves are brackish water swamps where plant and animal life forms exist in great profusion; they strain nutrients out of fresh water flowing to the sea, protect coastlines against erosion, and offer a sheltered nursery for young fish and birds.)[25]

Shrimp and shellfish farming along the coasts of tropical nations is destroying the world's mangrove forests. Ecuador, for example, was once bordered on the Pacific side with a plush belt of mangroves. Of the nation's original 177,000 hectares of mangroves, as many as 100,000 hectares are now producing shrimp, most of which are sold to the United States and Japan. Indonesia, Panama, and the Philippines are also steadily losing coastal forests to export-shrimp production. Offshore, meanwhile, prized fish species are pursued relentlessly. In the Atlantic, bluefin tuna—a favorite in Japan—are heading for extinction; their population fell from some 250 million in 1970 to perhaps 20,000 in 1990. Similarly, a rage for Cajun-style blackened red fish in the United States in the eighties has endangered spawning populations in the Gulf of Mexico.[26]

Fighting the trend to longer-distance food transport, communities in some industrial countries are finding creative ways to reforge connections with local farmers, strengthening city dwellers' sense that they are bound to the environment they inhabit. Farm markets, common in the Third World, are experiencing a renaissance in industrial countries. Massachusetts has worked with neighborhood and small-farm groups to establish more than 60 farmers' markets in the state since the late seventies, while the number in New York State jumped tenfold in the eighties.[27]

Farmers' markets shorten the distance from field to table, thereby saving energy and reducing the need for packaging. They also typically reduce the waste of food by about one fifth, because people are often happy to buy irregularly shaped or sized produce from farmers that they would reject in the sterile aisles of a supermarket. Along the same lines, institutional cafeterias at Saint Olaf and Carleton Colleges in Minnesota and Hendrix College in Arkansas have followed the recommendations of student-led environmental audits and begun buying from local farms.[28]

On a larger scale, the Seikatsu Club Consumers' Co-operative of Japan links 170,000 families through local buying and sharing groups, and coordinates their purchases of hundreds of products from thousands of environmentally sound producers and organic farms. The Club, founded in 1965, now has dozens of centers in communities where members live, at which they offer services ranging from organic foods to child care.[29]

Attacking long-distance trucking head-on, the National Association of Railroad Passengers is lobbying the U.S. Congress to rewrite fuel taxes that subsidize trucks at the expense of other highway users and that put energy-efficient rail freight at a disadvantage. In all these ways, food activists and others in the consumer class are working to rejuvenate local supply lines similar to those that feed the world's middle-income class.[30]

If all the world's people nourished themselves with the consumer class's regimen of meat, heavily packaged and processed foods and drinks, and specialties transported great distances, we would use more energy just for food and drinks than we currently do for all purposes—along with other natural resources in equally mammoth quantities. The ultimate goal of reforming food and beverage systems worldwide, then, should not be to raise the poor and middle income into the consumer class but to bring about a convergence of the three groups. From the middle-income class would come the basic menu of an abundance of locally grown produce and clean drinking water. From the consumer class would come technologies such as small, super-efficient refrigerators, advanced cooking stoves, and hot water for washing. The result of such convergence would be healthier people and a healthier planet.[31]

# 6

## Clean
## Motion

Before the industrial age, the speeds at which fortunate and unfortunate traveled differed only as much as the average gait of horses differed from that of humans: the rich rode, the poor walked. And that dichotomy endured for centuries; as French philosopher Paul Valéry wrote early in this century, "Napoleon moved no faster than Julius Caesar." But the division has widened explosively over the past hundred years. Maximum speed soared as the affluent switched from horses to trains to automobiles to jet airplanes, adding fuel requirements with each substitution. The poor still walk, at about the same speed as always, but the affluent have accelerated from about 10 kilometers an hour, the speed of a horse, to about 1,000 kilometers per hour, the speed of a jet.[1]

The historical progression of the affluent roughly parallels the transportation patterns of the world's economic classes: the walking poor, the bicycle-train-and-bus-riding middle-income class, and the car-driving consumer class. The richest members of the consumer class, finally, form the global jet set. With each step up this ladder, the environment suffers an order of magnitude more air pollution from burning fuels. Walking and bicycling cause virtually no ecological ills, requiring no fuel besides the person's most recent meal. For urban travel, buses, subways, and trolleys use roughly one eighth as much energy to move someone a kilometer as private cars do. For long trips, trains and buses require a tenth the energy of commercial jets—and one twenty-seventh the energy of private planes.[2]

The walking poor, of course, have too little mobility. Many of them never go more than 100 kilometers from their birthplaces. Unable to get to jobs easily, attend school, reach health clinics, bring their complaints before government offices, or expand their horizons through the broadening experience of travel, they are severely hindered by the lack of transportation. They inhabit places such as Pilcomaya, the "River of Birds," an isolated windswept valley in the Andes. There, the necessity of traversing the expanses between the adobe huts of sheep herders and subsistence farmers on foot makes survival a struggle and social visits a rarity.[3]

The middle-income class, particularly in China, relies on bicycles for short trips. Kilometer for kilometer, bikes are cheaper than any other vehicles, costing less than $100 new in most of the Third World. Lightweight of necessity, bikes require small amounts of materials to manufacture and their simplicity makes repair relatively easy. Indian bike repairers set up shop on street corners throughout the country by spreading a mat and laying out a few tools.[4]

Where railways exist, the middle-income class takes

longer trips by train. The Indian and Chinese rail systems, for example, move millions of people every day, allowing them to migrate for work or carry goods to market. To the consumer class, these rail systems would seem crowded and inefficient, but they function remarkably well considering their low cost. Buses, along with vans, trucks, converted jeeps, and dozens of other makeshift conveyances, carry those in the middle-income class on the rest of their journeys.

Most of these trains and buses are wasteful, polluting, and dangerous compared with models now used in industrial countries: buses with dozens of people clinging to their sides pump black diesel smoke into the streets of Lagos, Karachi, Guatemala City, and hundreds of other cities. But collectively these antiquated vehicles form transportation systems that pollute far less than would equivalent fleets of private cars, and they provide the middle-income class with affordable access to jobs, schools, and stores.

The consumer class, by contrast, employs modes of transportation—the private automobile and the jet—that all the world's people cannot use without ruining the atmosphere and coating huge areas of land in pavement. We members of the consumer class do almost all the world's driving. In 1988, per capita use of cars exceeded 4,000 kilometers in North America and Western Europe, while in the developing countries for which data were available, per person auto use was at or below 1,000 kilometers. Japan, with its excellent bicycle-and-rail-based transportation system, fell in between, with 2,510 kilometers per capita. (See Table 6-1.)[5]

A car is found in nearly every household in North America and Australia, and in a large and growing share of West European ones too. In Japan, the share jumped

TABLE 6-1. *Automobile Use Per Capita, Selected Countries, 1988[1]*

| Country | Automobile Travel |
|---|---|
| | (vehicle-kilometers per capita) |
| United States | 8,870 |
| West Germany | 6,150 |
| United Kingdom | 4,730 |
| Italy | 4,030 |
| Japan | 2,510 |
| Argentina | 1,000 |
| Poland | 710 |
| South Korea | 210 |
| Thailand | 190 |
| Cameroon | 120 |

[1]Some countries are for earlier years.

SOURCE: See endnote 5.

from 20 percent in 1970 to 72 percent in 1988. The auto class is also expanding rapidly in Eastern Europe and in newly industrializing countries such as South Korea and Brazil. At the heights of the consumer class, families are adding second cars. At least two cars are already found in one fifth of French—and half of American—households. Indeed, two thirds of new houses in the United States have two-car garages.[6]

Around the world, the great marketing achievement of the auto industry has been to turn its machines into cultural icons. As French philosopher Roland Barthes writes, "Cars today are almost the exact equivalent of the great Gothic cathedrals . . . the supreme creation of an era, conceived with passion by unknown artists, and consumed in image if not in usage by a whole population which appropriates them as . . . purely magical object[s]."[7]

The skill of automobile marketers in pushing symbol over substance is evident in the popularity of high-performance vehicles among urbanites who rarely use the special features. In Japan and India, young professionals cultivate an outdoorsy image with option-loaded Range Rovers and Jeeps. In the United States, car buyers have gone looking for fuel-guzzling high-powered engines: the average time American cars take to accelerate to highway speed has fallen every year since 1982. American city dwellers are also buying pickup trucks as never before, despite a 25-percent penalty in fuel economy compared with passenger cars. Since the early seventies, such light trucks have tripled their share of auto sales, and now constitute 18 percent of all personal vehicles on the road. European roads are crowded with the large cars previously familiar only in North America, and sales of racy BMW automobiles rose tenfold during the eighties in Japan.[8]

Whether we drive luxury or compact cars, however, all of us in the auto class share the responsibility for a litany of woes. Our 450 million vehicles are directly responsible for a quarter-million traffic fatalities a year, at least 13 percent of global carbon emissions from fossil fuels, and larger shares of local air pollution, noise pollution, and acid rain.[9]

Fueling passenger cars accounts for more than one fourth of world oil consumption, and manufacturing them takes additional energy. Pumping that fuel from the earth endangers ecosystems wherever it is pursued. And as oil companies drain easy-to-reach fields, they increasingly drill offshore or in remote wildlands such as Alaskan tundra and Ecuadoran rain forest. Oil refining, meanwhile, ranks first among U.S. manufacturing industries in energy intensity and fourth in total toxic emissions.[10]

In 1990, a typical American car was built from 1,000 kilograms of iron, steel, and other metals and 100 kilograms of plastic, making the auto industry one of the country's leading consumers of metals and a substantial user of plastics. Metal and plastic production, like petroleum production, are high-impact enterprises, ranking second and fifth respectively among U.S. manufacturing industries in energy intensity. Metal production, meanwhile, is third in total toxic emissions.[11]

Beyond the pollution cars cause and the resources they absorb, accommodating them has profound impacts on land. In the United States, roads, parking lots, and other areas devoted to the car occupy half of urban space. And nationwide, pavement covers an area larger than the state of Georgia. Everywhere the automobile holds sway, pavement sweeps out across the land. Fields turn into parking lots and forests into motorways. From 1970 to 1988—long after much of the U.S. interstate highway system was complete—paved roads in North America lengthened by 61 percent. Over the same period, Western Europe more than doubled and Japan quintupled their paved kilometers.[12]

Cars also remold communities and the character of daily life, as cities sprawl, public transit atrophies, and suburban shopping centers multiply. Even workplaces have begun to scatter; just half the residents of the San Francisco Bay area, for example, now work in the town where they live. The greater mobility of the private car has the paradoxical effect of lengthening how far people go rather than saving them time. In the late eighties, for instance, time-use surveys found little difference in average commuting times in the car-heavy United States and the nearly car-less Soviet Union. Soviet citizens walked or took the bus a half-hour each way; Americans, living in distant suburbs, drove the same amount of time.[13]

The inevitable consequence of lengthening daily travel distances is visible in the spread out suburbs of North America and Australia, where going to work, to school, or to the movies by public transportation is all but impossible. Thus, the sprawl that cars induce makes them indispensable. Even in Japan, where public transit is still predominant, the influence of the automobile is felt. Vacationing by train is becoming increasingly difficult as restaurants, hotels, and other tourist facilities shift away from train stations and toward highways.[14]

For the consumer class, longer commutes, greater sprawl, and worsening congestion all translate into lots of time in the car: working Americans now spend nine hours a week behind the wheel. To make these homes-away-from-home more comfortable, car manufacturers and drivers pile on the options. Some 92 percent of new U.S. cars have air conditioning, up from 5 percent in 1960. Air conditioning increases by two thirds a car's contribution to climate change and adds ozone-depleting chlorofluorocarbons to the atmosphere. Compact disk players will likely be in most new cars by the end of the nineties, and microwave ovens and telephones may not be far behind. The logical conclusion of this trend is already evident in a phenomenon automotive analysts dub "carcooning," in which drivers turn their four-wheelers into electronic cocoons outfitted with coffee makers, fax machines, televisions, and other gadgetry of the modern home.[15]

Atop the auto class sit members of the global jet set,

who go farther, faster, and at higher environmental cost than any other group. Air travel is growing phenomenally: passenger numbers rose 5 percent annually in the late eighties, and by decade's end the world's airlines were selling more than a billion tickets a year. In 1990, travelers covered 1.8 trillion kilometers by air—52 times what people covered in 1950. And most of that travel was enjoyed by the small group able to afford regular trips by air. Just 4 million Americans, for example, take 41 percent of domestic flights.[16]

Air travel makes even driving seem gentle on the environment. Jets use 40 percent more fuel than cars to move each passenger a kilometer, and much air travel has come not at the expense of car trips but of train and bus trips, thereby substituting the most energy-intensive form of long-distance travel for the least. Although airplanes do not cause much air pollution on the ground where people might inhale it, they pollute voluminously at higher altitudes.[17]

Planes are responsible for almost 3 percent of carbon emissions worldwide from fossil fuels, and other emissions may greatly amplify their responsibility for global warming. European researchers such as Swiss chemist Robert Egli believe that nitrogen emitted at planes' cruising altitude triggers two dangerous chain reactions. The first creates "bad" ozone in the troposphere (where it is a potent greenhouse gas) and the second destroys "good" ozone in the stratosphere (where it shields the earth from harmful ultraviolet rays). Airplane travel, like private car travel, is so intensive in its use of resources and its pollution of the environment that a future in which all the world's people fly like the jet set appears a flight of fancy.[18]

By contrast, the bikes, buses, and trains of the middle-income class, if updated with the latest technologies and complemented with occasional use of cars and planes, appear capable of providing environmentally sound transportation for all. These modes of transportation are frugal in their use of resources and rapid enough to take people efficiently to their destinations. Reducing auto dependence, of course, would also mean reversing urban sprawl, because well-planned, compact communities are needed for residents to be able to do many errands on foot or bike.

The low-impact transportation alternative is already within reach for a few cities. In Sweden, Stockholm is laid out to encourage walking, bicycling, and, in the long winter, cross-country skiing. Continuous paths through parkland encircle many of the islands on which the city is built, and Stockholm's commercial district is laced with bicycle routes, wide sidewalks, and pedestrian zones. Buses move swiftly through the metropolis, and the national bus and rail depot is in the heart of the city. People commute not only by foot and cycle but even by kayak, through the city's dozens of channels and waterways. In auto-dependent North America, Portland and Toronto have both worked for two decades on containing sprawl, on getting people out of their cars, and on boosting bus and rail travel, with remarkable results in air quality and urban spirit. Like Stockholm, these cities demonstrate that the automobile is more a hindrance than a boon to civic life.[19]

Still, shifting the transportation system of the consumer class away from cars and airplanes toward bicycles, buses, and trains is a radical proposal. Only intense and well-organized popular pressure will bring such sweeping changes. Fortunately, thousands of people around the world are already engaged in the struggle.

When their number is measured in millions, change may come quickly.

Some campaign quietly, leading by example. Mark Skinner, a high school physics teacher in Boston, Massachusetts, sold his car in 1991 and now bikes 13 kilometers to work each day. Millions of others in the consumer class own cars but leave them behind, walking, bicycling, or riding public transit to and from work and other destinations. Some activists follow the example of Michael Replogle, a transportation planner in the state of Maryland who started an organization in the early eighties to ship used bicycles from the United States to health workers and teachers in the Third World. The national campaign he catalyzed has packed and shipped 7,000 donated bikes to Central America, Haiti, and southern Africa, helped set up bicycle shops there, and advised Third World governments on low-energy transportation strategies.[20]

Transportation reformers with an economic bent hone in on national tax codes, which often favor car drivers. Friends of the Earth (FOE)–U.K. is campaigning against the tax breaks that thousands of British corporations get for providing company cars to employees. Others work at the local or regional level. Local FOE chapters in the United Kingdom, for example, are pressing town councils to make explicit planning targets for reducing car traffic. Myra Alperson of Johannesburg, South Africa, is pushing such basics as educating drivers to share the road with cyclists, while Nancy Dutko of Boulder, Colorado—who fought so hard for pedestrian rights that the state eventually hired her as an in-house advocate—reviews transportation plans to be sure they accommodate human-powered travel. On curtailing air travel, Sweden is leading the industrial world. In 1989, the country began taxing airplanes 12 kronor ($2) for each kilogram of hydrocarbons or nitrogen oxides they emit.[21]

Some change-makers even push the boundaries of legality to get their message heard. Tooker Gomberg of Edmonton travels throughout Canada doing street theater in traffic jams. Wearing a gas mask and a white decontamination suit, he issues "pollution tickets" to drivers. Ricardo Neves of Rio de Janeiro organized a campaign that won promises from the city government to designate bicycle lanes on major thoroughfares. When the government stalled on implementation, Neves and his colleagues took charge themselves, staging a "bike in" and painting "pirate" bike lanes on the streets. Similarly, local residents blocked 30 thoroughfares in Hamburg, Germany, in September 1991 to emphasize their demand for slower speed limits, traffic restraints that favor pedestrians, and designated bus and bicycle lanes.[22]

Whatever their means, transport reformers share a vision of cities no longer dominated by the noise, pollution, and wastefulness of the automobile, cities in which cars are used less because they are needed less, where we work and shop close to home, take excursions by public transit, and travel longer distances mostly by train. Attracted by successes such as Stockholm and Toronto and haunted by the gridlock of Los Angeles and Mexico City, they are pushing an agenda that coincides with the goal of global convergence. We in the auto class would meet the walking class on the middle way, riding bicycles, buses, and trains.

# 7

# The Stuff
# of Life

Consumer societies are commonly labeled materialistic, but in a deeper sense they are the opposite. As poet and farmer Wendell Berry argues, materialistic people would care about—and care for—material things, not just consume them. "Our economy is such that we 'cannot afford' to take care of things: Labor is expensive, time is expensive, money is expensive, but materials—the stuff of creation—are so cheap that we cannot afford to take care of them."[1]

The way a society treats metals, chemicals, paper, and other materials is a fundamental determinant of its impact on the natural realm. The industries that extract and process raw materials, just like the energy industry, are among the most polluting, energy-intensive, and ecologically destructive of all human endeavors. Producing chemicals, minerals, wood, and paper accounts for nearly 15 percent of U.S. energy consumption, and producing just metals, chemicals, and paper accounts for 85 percent of U.S. industrial emissions of toxic substances. If materials are, in Berry's words, "the stuff of creation," then affluent nations—far from being too materialistic—are not materialistic enough.[2]

As income rises, the propensity to care for material things appears to decline. The billion mostly rural people at the bottom of the global economic ladder cannot afford to waste, subsisting as they do on materials gathered from the fields and forests where they live. Most of the things they use each day—about a half kilogram of grain, 1 kilogram of fuelwood, and fodder for their animals—are theoretically renewable resources. In practice, unfortunately, landlessness and population growth often push the poor into marginal ecosystems, where they overexploit forests, grasses, soils, and wildlife, further impoverishing both the environment and themselves.[3]

The material poor carefully guard their few industrial products—tools and utensils, a book or two, perhaps a plastic bowl—but they are deprived of most basic durable goods made from nonrenewable resources. They must manage without plastic water pipes, tin roofs, or carts with lightweight wheels and ball bearings, and they lack amenities such as radios, refrigerators, and cooking stoves. They commonly consume fewer than 10 kilograms each of steel and paper a year, and similarly small quantities of cement. (See Table 7-1.)[4]

Steel, paper, and cement are good proxies for overall materials use because they make up a substantial share of the total, and all three are produced at considerable environmental cost. Steel production dominates the

TABLE 7-1. *Per Capita Consumption of Steel, Paper, and Cement in Selected Countries, Late Eighties*[1]

| Country | Steel | Paper | Cement[2] |
|---|---|---|---|
| | | (kilograms) | |
| Japan | 582 | 222 | 665 |
| Soviet Union | 582 | 36 | 470 |
| West Germany | 457 | 207 | 476 |
| United States | 417 | 308 | 284 |
| Turkey | 149 | 8 | 436 |
| Brazil | 99 | 27 | 167 |
| Mexico | 93 | 40 | 257 |
| China | 64 | 15 | 185 |
| Indonesia | 21 | 5 | 73 |
| India | 20 | 3 | 53 |
| Nigeria | 8 | 1 | 31 |
| Bangladesh | 5 | 1 | 3 |

[1]Steel, 1987; paper, 1989; cement, 1990. [2]Per capita production.

SOURCE: See endnote 4.

metals sector, using more than 90 percent by weight of all metals mined worldwide. Cement, beyond the high energy intensity of its production and the 2.5 percent of global carbon emissions that result from chemical reactions during its production, reflects the use of large quantities of construction materials quarried and hauled at high ecological cost. Paper mills, also energy-intensive, are heavy polluters of both air and water, releasing, among other things, dioxins that are among the most toxic known substances.[5]

Like the poor, members of the middle-income class are frugal in their use of materials. Their modest dwellings and vehicles, their ceiling fans, kitchen sinks, and other durable goods, and their newspapers and comic books are provided from less than 150 kilograms each of steel and cement and less than 50 kilograms of paper a year. While they use products antiquated by western standards—the ceiling fans squeak, the faucets drip—they suffer few real hardships for lack of things. And their thoroughness in reusing and recycling materials defines the ideal for all societies that aim to balance their economy with the environment. Rag pickers, junk dealers, scrap collectors, dairy deliverers, and a host of other tradespeople keep used objects in service. The economy of the middle-income class values stuff.[6]

At the top of the world economic ladder, consumption of materials swells dramatically, partly as people accumulate more goods, but mostly as waste proliferates. We consumers live in a materials economy dominated by excessive packaging, disposable products, rapid obsolescence, unrepairable goods, and mercurial fashions. As philosopher Ivan Illich wrote in 1977, "Industrial society has created an urban landscape that is unfit for people unless they devour each day their own weight in metals and fuels." Average Americans in the early nineties consume, either directly or indirectly, 52 kilograms of basic materials a day—18 kilograms of petroleum and coal, 13 of other minerals, 12 of agricultural products, and 9 of forest products.[7]

Daily consumption at these levels translates into global impacts that rank with the forces of nature. In 1990, mines scouring the crust of the earth to supply the consumer class moved more soil and rock than did all the world's rivers combined. The chemicals industry produced millions of tons of synthetic substances— more than 70,000 varieties—many of which have proved impossible to isolate from the natural environment. Scientists studying Antarctic snow, deep ocean fish, and subterranean water flows find traces of human-made chemicals.[8]

In the throwaway economy, packaging becomes an end in itself. Hardware supplies, children's toys, cosmetics, toiletries, pharmaceuticals, music recordings, food and drinks (as described in Chapter 5), and every other conceivable consumable is mounted on cardboard, wrapped in paper, sealed with plastic, or subjected to all three. Toy companies selling plastic playthings they claim are all but unbreakable cradle everything in plastic boxes four times the products' size. Gift wrap itself comes elaborately wrapped. Comedienne Lily Tomlin summed up this absurdity with a personal anecdote, "The other day I bought a waste basket and I carried it home in a paper bag, and when I got home I put the paper bag in the waste basket."[9]

Such excess explains why 4¢ of every dollar Americans spend on goods goes to packaging—$225 per person a year. It also explains the colossal quantities of resources devoted to wrappings. The industry absorbs 5 percent of energy in the United Kingdom, 40 percent of paper in Germany, and nearly a fourth of plastics in the United States. In industrial countries, where most of the consumer class lives, packaging makes up close to half the volume of municipal solid waste. The wrapping boom is catching on in poor countries as well: China's emerging packaging industry quadrupled sales in the eighties.[10]

Like packaging, disposables proliferate in the consumer society. From kitchen plates to cameras, the consumer economy substitutes transient throwaways for durable goods that exemplify environmentally sound living. The British dump 2.5 billion diapers a year. The Japanese use 30 million "disposable" single-roll cameras annually, and Japanese corporations hand out millions of free batteries—each containing toxic cadmium and mercury—in addition to their old-fashioned promotional disposable pens. Americans annually discard 183 million razors, 2.7 billion batteries, 140 million cubic meters of styrofoam packing "peanuts," 350 million pressurized spray paint cans, plus enough paper and plastic ware to feed the world a picnic every other month. One company in Maryland even sells throwaway videocassettes, made to be junked after 5-10 playings.[11]

The throwaway economy also undermines durability. What economists call "consumer durables"—home appliances, for example—are not in fact particularly durable. Tinkerer Tim Hunkin spent two years poking around waste sites in England studying discarded household appliances. His findings reveal the prevailing trend toward planned obsolescence and disposability: "The machines that date back to the 1950s are very solid, made mostly of metal with everything bolted or welded together. As the years passed, machines have become more flimsy. More parts are now made of plastic, and they are glued together rather than welded or bolted. . . . Many parts are now impossible to repair. . . . New machines are so cheap that it frequently does not pay to have a faulty appliance repaired professionally."[12]

A more rigorous study of European household appliances found that their longevity has at best stayed level over the decades, despite steady gains on every other measure of product quality. New refrigerators, for example, cost less, hold more, and use less energy than their predecessors, but they do not last any longer. The simple reason is that manufacturers design them to last a certain period and then be replaced instead of repaired.

From a narrow economic perspective, planned obsolescence is a logical response to the relative costs of production—labor is expensive, and mass production takes less time per worker than repair. But from a broader perspective, it reflects the consumer economy's low esteem for the earth. As Berry said, under the prevailing economic values, the stuff of creation is too cheap to care for.[13]

The same forces that make repair difficult also work against the recycling of materials locked up in large goods. In the past, Japanese appliance makers collected most used units for scrap, but they are reluctant to do so now: new models have so many unreusable plastic parts that scrapping no longer pays off. So the consumer class's refuse heaps are full of consumer durables. Each year, we in the throwaway class discard millions of desks, chairs, tables, cabinets, refrigerators, air conditioners, clothes washers, clothes dryers, personal computers, telephones, answering machines, and mattresses. Germans alone throw away 5 million household appliances a year, and Americans toss 7.5 million television sets. Only one fourth of the 280 million tires Americans throw out each year are recycled or retreaded.[14]

Where disposability and planned obsolescence fail to accelerate the trip from cash register to junk heap, fashion sometimes succeeds. Oscar Wilde once asked, "What is fashion? . . . It is usually a form of ugliness so intolerable that we have to alter it every six months"; fashion has only accelerated since his time. High fashion changed every two-and-a-half months in the late eighties, according to the U.S. Office of Technology Assessment, but most clothing, whether high fashion or low, goes out of style long before it is worn out. As a marketing analyst said 25 years ago, "Every industry tries to emulate the woman's fashion industry. This is the key to modern marketing."[15]

Lately, the kingdom of fashion has colonized watches and eyeglasses, as marketers offered styles to go with any outfit, and has invaded the realm of sports footwear. Kevin Ventrudo, chief financial officer of California-based L.A. Gear, which saw sales multiply fiftyfold in four years, told the *Washington Post*, "If you talk about shoe performance, you only need one or two pairs. If you're talking fashion, you're talking endless pairs of shoes." The result of foot fetishism among urban youths, fed by annual advertising expenditures on the order of $200 million, is that teenagers account for 30 percent of shoe sales.[16]

Admittedly, making apparel and footware takes nothing like the toll on the earth that heavy industries do, but supplying the fashion market does entail some ecological damage. Cotton farmers are some of the world's heaviest users of pesticides and water. Synthetic fabrics originate in the petrochemical industry. Some wool and leather comes from livestock on overgrazed range. And textile mills use industrial dyes that register as hazardous substances.[17]

So we consumers would do well to follow some advice from an unexpected quarter. The San Francisco-based clothing firm Esprit ran advertisements in late 1990 under the headline A Plea for Responsible Consumption: "Today, more than ever, our lifestyles must address the ever-increasing threats to our environment. We believe this can best be achieved by asking ourselves before we buy something, whether it is something we really need. By taking this approach, we'll contribute to a healthier attitude about consumption. This may sound like heresy from an apparel manufacturer, but if this kind of commitment doesn't catch on quickly, we could devour all that's left on the planet."18

The upper echelon of the consumer class—the rich—have reached the pinnacle of materials consumption and joined the gilded class. To them falls responsibility for the rampant despoliation caused by mining precious metals and gems. Such materials are unique in the destruction involved in securing even small quantities of them, and in the fact that their value is intangible, even artificial. Precious metals and gems are precious only because people prize them, and they are dug up primarily to be hoarded away.

This intangible value to the few has dire tangible results for the environment. Nearly 1,000 tons of mercury have infiltrated the Amazon food chain since the early eighties as Brazilian miners have used the deadly metal to separate gold from sediment. The ultimate victims may be the native tribes who hunt and fish for survival. South African gold mines seep radioactive radon gas into black townships, and diamond mines in Botswana are draining the Okavango Delta, a vast wildlife sanctuary little disturbed—so far—by human intervention. Compared with the gilded class, even the throwaway consumers walk softly on the earth.19

Ironically, in today's consumer class, environmental advocates must introduce as new such practices as "reuse" and "recycling"—practices that thrived not so long ago. Only after four decades of binge consumption could thrift seem an innovation. Caring for things is a part of the cultural legacy of all societies, including the industrial nations that now consume so much. Laura Ingalls Wilder, for example, in her classic children's book *Little House on the Prairie*, described the true materialism that prevailed among earlier generations of

Americans. When her father shingled the roof of their prairie house, Laura stood below and carefully collected any nails that might tumble down. Not a single nail was to be wasted.[20]

Such time-honored values, which persist lower on the economic ladder, need rejuvenating among us in the consumer society if the world's people are to converge on a middle path of materials use. A future that joined the advanced low-resource technologies of affluent nations—fiber optic cables and laptop computers—with the conserving values and emphasis on durable goods of the middle-income class would combine the best of both worlds. It would meld many of the comforts enjoyed by the consumer class with levels of per capita materials use common in the middle-income class. But such a future will depend on widening the movement against waste.

Fortunately, from the subsidized industries at the top of the materials stream to the manufacturers in the middle and the waste heaps at the end, there are as many opportunities for change—for revaluing the stuff of creation—as there are people to take up the task. American Phil Hocker works at the top. After a decade pushing reforms of U.S. mining regulation, he was ready in 1989 to launch a frontal assault on the General Mining Act of 1872, a law that virtually gives away public land to prospectors, thereby suppressing minerals prices. His movement has not yet won, but American mining interests are on the defensive as never before.[21]

In the forests of North America, which provide the largest share of the consumer class's wood and paper, reform movements are afoot as well. In 1989, Jeff Debonis, then an 11-year employee of the U.S. Forest Service, founded the Association of Forest Service Employees for Environmental Ethics, a group that aims to transform the bureaucracy from within by supporting "whistle blowers"—employees who call attention to violations of environmental guidelines. In Canada, Cree Indian Louise Sinclair is struggling to arrest the clear-cutting of northern forests on Cree lands.[22]

Further down the materials stream, Dieter Rams of the German consumer products company Braun blazes the trail for other product designers by engineering simpler, more-durable clocks, calculators, and kitchen appliances. Says Rams, "We have too many things in our lives. There is too much clutter, too much visual and material pollution. One of the main challenges for industrial designers is to create products with longer life-cycles so we can buy fewer things."[23]

In curtailing material waste, Germans lead the consumer class. Environmental advocates won a stunning victory in 1991 when environment minister Klaus Töpfer introduced a comprehensive plan to reduce packaging waste. By 1995, German industry will have to collect and reuse or recycle most packaging materials, including cardboard, paper, plastic, glass, and metal, along with many large consumer goods such as automobiles and home appliances. The plan, which also involves stiff waste fees, essentially makes German industries responsible for caring for the materials they use, even after they have sold them as products and packaging to buyers.[24]

At the tail of the materials stream is one of fastest-brewing grassroots environmental fights in the United States. As municipality after municipality fills its landfill sites, many of them have planned massive waste incinerators—incinerators that pollute the air and, despite the electricity they generate, are net losers of energy. By burning things that could be recycled, incinerators drive the energy-guzzling raw materials industries to higher levels of production. Ellen and Paul Connett of Canton, New York, are in the front lines of the battle against incinerators, arming local groups across the country with the facts through their homegrown newsletter, *Waste Not.* Community groups in Washington State who won the recycling-or-incinerators struggle in 1988 can now boast that Seattle recycles 40 percent of its solid waste, the most of any large U.S. city.[25]

Less confrontational is the strategy of Briton Glyn Roberts, who years ago began collecting and refurbishing old hand tools and shipping them to material-poor African artisans. His personal efforts grew into a nationwide British organization called Tools for Self Reliance. The movement's 50 U.K. chapters, plus members in the Netherlands, Germany, and Scandinavia, have shipped 250,000 implements and helped local groups establish tool-making facilities in East Africa. Roberts understands that millions of high-quality chisels, saws, and hoes in the hands of poor workers help them more than the few power machines that official aid programs provide.[26]

While the throwaway economy persists, some activists use its wastes to make a point—and a profit. Everything Goes Furniture collects, refurbishes, and sells furniture people dump on the streets of New York City. Urban Ore of Berkeley, California, has a warehouse and sorting center at the city dump, and contracts with the city to sort valuables out of the trash flow. They sell what they find at a store next door. Uniting such scavenging entrepreneurs nationwide is their trade association, the National Association of Dumpster Divers and Urban Miners.[27]

Regardless of where on the materials stream they concentrate, all these efforts manifest the kind of true materialism we so need in the consumer class. Curbing waste, conserving and repairing things, reusing and recycling materials: caring for the earth means caring for the things we take from it.

# III

---

# Taming
# Consumerism

---

# 8

# The Myth of
# Consume or Decline

Received wisdom in the consumer society holds that, regardless of consumption's human and environmental effects, we must pursue it as a matter of national policy in order to keep ourselves employed. This assumption runs deep. Broadcast news programs cover retail districts in the holiday season as if they were scenes of national significance, offering commentary on shoppers' readiness to spend. When recession hit the United States in mid-1990, everyone from the president on down began begging loyal Americans to spend. Range Rover bought full-page advertisements in major U.S. periodicals pleading, "Buy Something. Our preference, of course, would be that you buy a Range Rover. But if that's not in the cards, buy a microwave. A basset hound. Theater tickets. A Tootsie Roll. Something."[1]

The reasoning behind such entreaties sounds impeccable: if no one buys, no one sells, and if no one sells, no one works. Thus, in the consumer economy—where two thirds of gross national product consists of consumer expenditures—everything from fortunes on the stock market to national economic policies hinges on surveys of "consumer confidence" and "intentions to buy." If this consume-or-decline view is right, then lowering our consumption on purpose, individually and collectively, would be self-destructive. If it is true, then cutting our driving in half, for example, would throw half the gasoline station attendents out of work, along with half the car mechanics, auto workers, tire factory workers, auto insurance agents, and car financing specialists. The shock of those layoffs rippling through the economy would cause a chain reaction of additional job losses that could end in a repeat of the Great Depression.[2]

Mainstream development economists paint a similarly nightmarish scenario for developing countries. The industrial countries, they solemnly intone, are the locomotive of the world economy. If we consumers shifted away from junk food, cars, and disposables, we would need fewer of the products of the middle income and the poor. Contracting demand in industrial countries would leave impoverished lands stranded in destitution. Having gambled everything on consumers' endlessly growing appetite for their raw materials exports, developing nations would fall into irreversible decline. In this view, failing to increase consumer-class intake of raw materials is a crime against the 42 poorest nations—what the United Nations calls the least developed countries—because they depend on commodity exports for more than 60 percent of their foreign earnings.[3]

The consume-or-decline argument contains a grain of truth. The global economy is indeed structured primarily to feed the consumer life-style of the world's affluent fifth. And shifting from high to low consumption would shake that structure to its core. It would require legions of workers to change jobs, whole continents to restructure their industrial bases, and enterprises of all scales to transform their operations. It would, worst of all, entail painful dislocation for thousands of families and communities.

But those who defend this argument ignore the alternative: continuing to pillage and poison the earth would guarantee not only the same misfortunes but worse. Fishers will be left idle if water pollution and overharvesting decimate fisheries. Farmers will abandon their fields if recurrent drought kills their crops and animals. Loggers will have little to do if the forests die from air pollution, acid rain, and shifting climatic zones. Carmakers and home builders will not find many buyers if people must spend most of their earnings on scarce food supplies. Business, in short, will not do well on a dying planet. In this light, the fact that some workers would lose jobs is no more an argument against lowering consumption than job losses in the weapons industry are an argument against peace.

If we attempt to preserve the consumer economy indefinitely, ecological forces will dismantle it savagely. If we proceed to dismantle it gradually ourselves, we will have the opportunity of replacing it with a low-consumption economy that can endure—an economy of permanence.

Such a transition will be challenging, but perhaps less so than the consume-or-decline argument suggests, because that line of thought rests on three arguable assumptions. First, it assumes that consumption of economic services as denominated in dollars is immutably bonded to consumption of physical resources in the economy. Second, it assumes that employment is equally bonded to flows of physical resources. (Because of these two assumptions, consume-or-decline thinking disregards the perverse effects of current subsidy and taxation systems, which boost resource consumption at the expense of employment.) Third, it assumes a model of employment—year-round work, 40 hours a week— that requires more daily hours than have most civilizations in history.

Physical flows of natural resources would fall radically in an economy of permanence, while the money value of the services that people enjoy might fall little. The crucial distinction is between physical commodities and the services people use those commodities to get. For example, nobody wants telephone books, newspapers, or magazines for their own sake; rather, we want access to the information they contain. In an economy of permanence, that information might be available to us for much the same price on durable electronic readers. That would enable us to consult the same texts but eliminate most paper manufacturing and the associated pollution.

Likewise, people do not want cars as such; they buy them to gain ready access to a variety of facilities and locations. Good town planning and public transportation could provide that access equally well. In every sector of the economy, from housing to food, this distinction between means (physical goods) and ends (services) helps lay bare the vast opportunities to disconnect high resource consumption from quality of life.

By the same token, the total amount of work done in

an economy of permanence may decrease little compared with the shrinking flows of natural resources because the most ecologically damaging products and forms of consumption also usually generate the fewest jobs. Indeed, there is a striking correspondence between high labor intensity and low environmental impact. Repairing existing products, for example, uses more labor and fewer resources than manufacturing new ones would. Railway systems employ more people but fewer natural resources than comparable fleets of cars do. Improving energy efficiency employs more people than boosting energy production would. And recycling programs employ more people than waste incinerators or landfills do.[4]

Were the consumer class to move toward the life-style sketched in Part II—substituting local foods for grain-fed meat and packaged fare, switching from cars to bikes and buses, and replacing throwaways with durable goods—labor-intensive industries would benefit greatly. Still, on balance, the amount of paid work done might decrease, because low-impact industries would probably expand less than high-impact industries contracted. To cope fairly with slackening job markets, societies would have to shorten working hours per person; fortunately, as discussed later in this chapter, most of us consumers work more than we wish to anyway.

The crucial employment question is how to manage the transition to low consumption. The challenge for governments will be to lead the conversion of the economy to environmental sustainability by providing laborers in high-impact fields with sufficient job retraining to switch careers, by offering adequate unemployment compensation to smooth the process, and by pioneering new models of reduced and flexible working hours.

Governments also face the challenge of radically reorienting prevailing tax and subsidy policies, many of which promote the worst kinds of consumption. Most nations, for example, favor the auto, energy, mining, timber, and grain-fed livestock industries with a long list of tax write-offs and direct subsidies. The United States virtually gives away minerals on federal land, builds logging roads into national forests at taxpayer expense, and sells irrigation water in the arid West at a loss. France massively subsidizes its nuclear power complex, Russia its oil industry, the United Kingdom its auto drivers, the Canadian province of Quebec its aluminum smelters, and Japan its feedgrain growers.[5]

Beyond financial transfers and biased policies are the implicit subsidies of the nature-blind economic accounting systems that governments use. Land use and materials policies in most of the world undervalue renewable resources, ignore natural services provided by ecosystems, and therefore underprice raw materials extracted from the public domain. Coal and oil are not priced to reflect the damage their production and combustion cause to human health and natural ecosystems. Pulp and paper are not priced to reflect the habitat destroyed and water poisoned in their production. Scores of products—from toxic chemicals to excessive packaging—cost the earth more than their price tags reveal; where outright bans or strict regulation are inappropriate, they should be taxed accordingly.[6]

If goods' prices reflected something closer to their full environmental costs, through comprehensive revisions of subsidies and taxes, the market would help guide consumers toward lower resource consumption. Disposables and packaging, for instance, would rise in price relative to durable, less-packaged goods; local unprocessed food would fall in price relative to prepared products trucked from far away. If legislators shifted the tax burden from labor to resources, companies would swiftly move to trim resource use as environmental taxes rose, and hire more people as income taxes fell.[7]

Already, environmental and taxpayer groups in many nations single out egregious subsidies and tax shelters as targets for reform. But they commonly lose the big battles, overwhelmed by the political clout of the billion-dollar industries that doggedly defend the status quo. In early 1992, for example, European energy interests were waging a successful war on a proposal to tax carbon emissions in the European Community. Every battle lost demonstrates the difficulty and the urgency of mobilizing more members of the consumer class in support of prices that try to tell the ecological truth.[8]

Equally debatable is the consume-or-decline argument's contention that the world's poor cannot afford for us consumers to live on less. Although many developing countries and regions within them are integrated into the world economy as suppliers of raw materials, this situation puts them in a dependent status that their leaders have decried for decades. To date, furthermore, the trickle-down effects of the growing consumer economy have proved a disappointing source of economic stimulus for the poor. Indeed, the most notable consequence so far has been to create enclaves of world-class consumers in every nation.

These elites profit mightily from the exports of natural resources from the global South to the global North. But the world's poor have gained little beyond devastated homelands. Ending poverty, as innumerable experts confirm, depends mainly on national programs and policies designed explicitly for that purpose. It depends on aggressive national campaigns for basic health, education, and family planning, on broad-based labor-intensive development schemes in rural areas, on the mobilizing efforts of grassroots organizations, and on the existence of responsive local and national governments. To finance all these, it depends on economic policies that promote innovation, reward success, and allow markets to work efficiently. But it does not necessarily depend on production of bulky, low-value goods destined for export to the consumer class.[9]

More beneficial to the middle income and poor of the world than increased consumer-class consumption would be world trade rules that were written so as to make commodity prices reflect more of the ecological costs of production. If Malaysia, Chile, and Kampuchea, for example, were in a position to charge Japanese buyers for the ecological destruction associated with cutting down ancient forests, they could earn the foreign currency they need while felling fewer trees.[10]

Just like the high-impact sectors of the industrial world, resource-extracting regions of the world will face a severe test in the transition away from supplying the consumer society. And like the vulnerable workers of high-impact industries of the North, their people will need a helping hand to make it through. We consumers can assist with financial and technical resources, and with support for their grassroots projects and struggles. But in the end, the poor and middle-income families whose livelihoods are currently linked to the consumer class's consumption must chart their own destiny.

Reforming subsidies and taxes and refocusing development on ending poverty would mark important strides toward an economy of permanence. A third crucial reform is for us consumers to release ourselves from the strictures of full-time work. More and more of us find ourselves agreeing with American industrial designer William Stumpf, who says, "We've got enough stuff. We need more time."[11]

Although fulfilling work and adequate leisure are both key determinants of human contentment, the balance in the consumer society tilts too far toward work. Working hours in industrial societies, although far below their peak during the Industrial Revolution, remain high by historical standards. Japanese and Americans are especially overworked. Europeans have been trading part of their pay raises for additional leisure time since 1950, but Americans and Japanese have not.[12]

In Germany and France, the average hours worked per week has gone from 44 and 38 hours respectively in 1950 to 31 hours in 1989, with much of the decline reflecting annual vacation leaves spanning four to eight weeks. In Japan, weekly hours have gone from 44 to 41. In the United States, meanwhile, the workweek declined slightly from 1950 to 1970, but has actually increased since then. Americans work 38 hours a week, on average, and have added an entire month's worth of work to their schedule since 1970.[13]

Harvard University economist Juliet Schor writes in *The Overworked American*: "Since 1948, the level of productivity of the U.S. worker has more than doubled. In other words, we could now produce our 1948 standard of living in less than half the time. Every time productivity increases, we are presented with the possibility of either more free time or more money. We could have chosen the four-hour day. Or a working year of six months. Or every worker in the United States could now be taking every other year off from work—with pay." Instead, Americans work the same hours and earn twice the money.[14]

To check whether that choice reflected the will of

American workers, Schor delved into the arcane field of labor-market economics and, having surveyed dozens of studies, concluded it did not. Workers in all the core regions of the consumer society express—either in opinion surveys or in collective bargaining positions—a strong desire for additional leisure time and a willingness to trade pay increases for it. They also report that they do not have that option. They can take a job or leave it, but they cannot take it for fewer hours a day. Part-time work, furthermore, is in general less skilled, less interesting, and less well paid because it lacks fringe benefits such as retirement and insurance plans. So most of us are left with the choice of good full-time jobs or bad part-time ones.[15]

Although cynics predict shorter workdays would simply translate into more time watching television, there is abundant reason to believe otherwise. For many people, television is something to do when their creative energy is low, when they are too tired to do something more rewarding. Europeans both work less and watch less television than Americans; Japanese both work more and watch more television. In an earlier era, cynics said workers would squander free time on drinking and gambling, but when the W.K. Kellogg Company shortened its workday from eight hours to six during the Great Depression in the United States, community initiatives proliferated. Contemporary observer Henry Goddard Leach noticed "a lot of gardening and community beautification. . . . Athletics and hobbies were booming. . . . Libraries [were] well patronized . . . and the mental background of these fortunate workers . . . [was] becoming richer."[16]

As a first step in letting Americans begin enjoying the rewards of high productivity, Schor calls for legal bans on mandatory overtime for wage earners and for requirements that firms stick to stated work hours for salaried staff members, compensating them for any extra hours with an equal amount of paid time off. She suggests making part-time work more feasible by requiring that part-time employees get benefits prorated to their hours of work. Finally, she recommends labor laws that make the choice between time and money explicit.[17]

Mounting pressure for more time instead of more money is evident in things like the campaign of some 240 U.S. labor, women's, and children's organizations for the right to take time off for family and medical purposes. The coalition, chaired by the Women's Legal Defense Fund, pushed a bill through both houses of Congress in 1991 that was later vetoed by President Bush. Similarly, for two decades unions such as Service Employees International have been urging managers to introduce voluntary work-time reduction programs, under which workers can cut back their hours somewhat when they want free time instead of money. The Service Employees won such a program temporarily for California State government workers in the seventies, and later prevailed permanently for New York State government employees.[18]

More recently, according to Barney Olmsted, co-director of the California-based nonprofit New Ways to Work, interest has surged in flexible work arrangements such as job sharing, particularly among women stretched thin by the "double day" of career and family. Eastman Kodak is one of several major corporations that now allow employees to plan periods of part-time work into their careers. So far, unfortunately, American men have not joined women in pushing for flexible or reduced hours, because, Olmsted says, society puts "a

real stigma on men who don't want to work full time."
Meanwhile, in Japan, where *karoshi* (death from over-
work) kills perhaps 10,000 people a year, young workers
are displaying a newly disapproving attitude to overtime, pressuring colleagues to leave the office at the end
of the scheduled day. The Japanese government plans to
switch the country from a six-day workweek to a five-
day one by early in the next century. In Europe, too,
unions continue to press for additional time off.[19]

No one can say yet how strong this preference for free
time over extra consumption is. In theory, if everyone
consistently chose free time over additional money, nor-
mal gains in labor productivity would cut consumer-
class working hours in half by 2020, giving us abundant
time for personal development and for family and community activities.[20]

The world economy is currently organized to furnish
1.1 billion people with a consumer life-style long on
things but short on time. The prospect of restructuring
that economy is daunting, but the consume-or-decline
argument, which holds high consumption indispensable
for employing workers and combatting deprivation, is
ungrounded. High consumption is a precondition to
neither full employment nor the end of poverty. And
many consumers appear ready to say enough is enough,
so long as they get more free time out of the bargain.

# 9

# The Cultivation
# of Needs

"Fifty years ago," wrote philosopher Ivan Illich in 1977, "most of the words an American heard were personally spoken to him as an individual, or to someone standing nearby." Today, the same can hardly be said. Most of the words an American or any of us in the global consumer society hears are sales pitches broadcast over the airwaves to us as part of a mass market. The text we read, the images we see, and the public places we visit are all dominated by commercial messages crafted to arouse our appetites. In particular, advertising, commercial television, and shopping centers all potently promote consumerism. For those seeking to live within the means of the earth, challenging all three must be a high priority.[1]

Communications in the consumer society is dominated by the sales pitch, by the unctuous voices of the marketplace. Advertising is everywhere, bombarding typical members of the consumer class with some 3,000 messages a day, according to *Business Week*. Ads are broadcast by thousands of television and radio stations, towed behind airplanes, plastered on billboards and in sports stadiums, and bounced around the planet from satellites. They are posted on chair-lift poles on ski slopes, hung on banners at televised parades and festivals, piped into classrooms and doctors' offices, weaved into the plots of feature films, and stitched onto Boy Scout merit badges and professional athletes' jerseys.[2]

Advertisers have a brave new world in mind, full of technologies putting them within striking distance wherever we consumers go. They have begun erecting wall-sized video screens in malls to heighten the frenzy of the shopping experience. They install ad-packed closed-circuit television systems at airports, bus stops, subway stations, exercise clubs, ski resorts, and supermarket checkout lines. Food engineers have even begun turning the food supply into a vehicle for ads. The Viskase company of Chicago prints edible slogans on hot dogs, and Eggverts International is using a similar technique to advertise on thousands of eggs in Israel. Demonstrating that not even the sky is the limit, Coca-Cola convinced orbiting Soviet cosmonauts to sip their soft drink on camera in August 1991. Billed an "experiment" by the company, the event was the first commercial filmed in outer space.[3]

No market can function smoothly where buyers lack information about the goods and services offered; advertising, according to orthodox economic theory, provides that information. But the contents of marketing messages themselves show the simplemindedness of that explanation. As dozens of similar products compete for buyers' allegiance, advertisements increasingly resemble dreams. Many ads offer little information, trafficking instead in images evoking sexual virility, eternal youth, existential fulfillment, and infinite other variations on the "wouldn't-you-like-to-be-like-this" theme. Television advertisements have become so image-laden that some viewers have fun playing a game called "guess the product": automobile ads may show only clouds and waves, cigarette ads only models in swim suits. Peter Kim, director of research and consumer behavior for the marketing firm J. Walter Thompson, says the role of brands in consumer society is "much akin to the role of myth in traditional societies. Choosing a brand becomes a way for one group of consumers to differentiate themselves from another."[4]

The barrage of sales spiels is so intense in the consumer society that people actually remember few ads. Yet commercials have an effect nonetheless. Even if they fail to sell a particular product, they sell consumerism itself by ceaselessly reiterating the idea that there is a product to solve each of life's problems, indeed that existence would be satisfying and complete if only we bought the right things. Advertisers thus cultivate needs by hitching their wares to the infinite existential yearnings of the human soul.[5]

Entire industries have manufactured a need for themselves. Writes one advertising executive, ads can serve "to make [people] self-conscious about matter of course things such as enlarged nose pores [and] bad breath." Advertisers especially like to play on the personal insecurities and self-doubt of women. As B. Earl Puckett, then head of the Allied Stores Corporation, put it 40 years ago, "It is our job to make women unhappy with what they have." Thus for those born with short, skinny eyelashes, the message mongers offer hope. For those whose hair is too straight, or too curly, or grows in the wrong places, for those whose skin is too dark or too light, for those whose body weight is distributed in anything but this year's fashion, advertising assures us that synthetic salvation is close at hand.[6]

The cultivation of needs is a mammoth global enterprise. For four decades, advertising has been one of the world's fastest-growing industries. In the United States, ad expenditures rose from $198 per capita in 1950 to $495 in 1990. Total global advertising expenditures, meanwhile, rose from an estimated $39 billion in 1950 to $247 billion in 1988, growing far more rapidly than economic output. Over the same period, per person expenditures grew from $15 to $47. (See Figure 9-1.) In developing countries, too, advertising has exploded. Ad billings in India jumped fivefold in the eighties, and South Korea's advertising industry grew 35-40 percent annually in the late eighties. The latest boom is now under way in Eastern Europe, a region that John Lindquist of the Boston Consulting Group calls "an advertising executive's dream—people actually remember advertisements."[7]

Marketers are increasingly targeting the young. One specialist in marketing to children told the *Wall Street Journal*, "Even two-year-olds are concerned about their brand of clothes, and by the age of six are full-out consumers." In Japan, where average parents lavish each child with $450 worth of toys and $770 worth of clothes a year, some gem shops specialize in jewelry for children younger than 12. Takayama Hideo, head of Tokyo's Children Research Institute, reports, "Today's mothers . . . want their infants dressed to match what they them-

1989 dollars

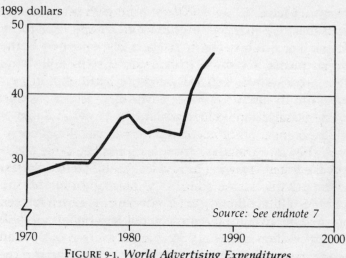

FIGURE 9-1. *World Advertising Expenditures Per Capita, 1970-88*

selves wear. They buy fancy tableware and other goods for their children and . . . they're more fashion conscious." Even in Malaysia, youngsters have absorbed a consumerist outlook. Notes social psychologist Chiam Heng Keng of Kuala Lumpur's University of Malaysia, children are "definitely more materialistic—to be 'with' the groups you have to buy certain things."[8]

The children's market in the United States is so valuable—topping $75 billion in 1990—that American companies spent $500 million marketing to it in 1990, five times more than they spent a decade earlier. They started cartoons centered around toys, and began direct-mail marketing to youngsters enrolled in their company-sponsored "clubs." Such saturation advertising has allowed some firms to stake huge claims in the children's market. Mattel vice president Meryl Friedman brags, "Mattel has achieved a stunning 95 percent penetration with Barbie [dolls] among girls age 3 to 11 in the U.S." Predictably, major retailers have opened Barbie departments to compete for the loyalty of doll-doting future consumers, and marketers pay premium prices to employ the dolls as an advertising medium. Barbies come equipped with Reebok shoes and Benetton clothes.[9]

Although advertising's main ecological danger is its promotion of consumerism, it also uses up lots of paper. Ads pack the daily mail—14 billion mail-order catalogs plus 38 billion other assorted ads clog the post each year in the United States. And they fill periodicals: a typical American newspaper is 65 percent advertising, up from 40 percent half a century ago. Every year, Canada cuts 17,000 hectares of its primeval forests—an area the size of the District of Columbia—just to provide American dailies with newsprint on which to run advertisements. As Colleen McCrory, one of a growing cadre of Canadians struggling to protect the nation's forest inheritance, puts it, "Basically, we're turning the whole nation into pulp."[10]

Considering how few people look at most of those ads, the environmental cost is extraordinary. Computer owner David Briars of Craftsbury, Vermont, for example, decided to calculate the price to the earth of the annoying computer supply catalogs that appeared in his mailbox. A series of phone calls later he had reached his conclusions: each year, making the paper for one company's bimonthly catalog, sent to 3 million people, takes wood from seven decades' worth of growth on 28 hectares of land, plus 590 million liters of water, and 23,000 megawatts of electric and steam power. The production process would release into the air or water 14 tons of sulfur dioxide and 345 tons of chlorinated organic compounds, a group of chemicals that includes some of the world's most toxic substances. Briars has now started a letter-writing campaign to stem the tide of catalogs.[11]

Restraining the excesses of marketers and limiting commercials to their legitimate role of informing consumers will require fundamental reforms in the industry, changes that will not come about without a well-organized grassroots movement. The advertising industry is a formidable foe and on the march around the world, but it is already vulnerable where it pushes products demonstrably dangerous to human health. Tobacco ads are or soon will be banished from television throughout the West, and alcohol commercials are under attack as never before.[12]

Another ready target for advertising activists is the assault that marketers make on children. Public sentiment runs strongly against marketing campaigns that prey on youngsters. Action for Children's Television, a citizens group based in Boston, won a victory in late 1990 when the U.S. Congress hemmed in television commercials aimed at children. The same year, public interest organizations in the European Community won standards on television for Europe after 1992 that will put strict limits on some types of ads.[13]

The Australian Consumers' Association is attacking junk food ads, calling for a ban or strict limits on hawking unhealthful fare to youngsters. Of food ads aired during children's television programs, the association's research shows 80 percent are for high-fat, high-salt, excessively packaged snacks. The American Academy of Pediatrics is similarly concerned. Noting the high proportion of advertisements for products that violate nutrition guidelines, the organization is urging Congress to ban food ads that target the young.[14]

Alternatively, consumers could take aim at trumped-up corporate environmental claims. Since 1989, marketers have been painting their products "green" in an attempt to tap citizen anger at corporate ecological transgressions. In 1990, for example, the oil company Texaco offered Americans "free" tree seedlings to plant for the good of the environment; to qualify, a customer had to buy eight or more gallons of gasoline. Unmentioned in the marketing literature was the fact that it takes a typical tree about four years to store as much carbon dioxide as is released in refining and burning eight gallons of fuel, and that most tree seedlings planted by amateurs promptly die.[15]

In the United States, one fourth of all new household products introduced in 1990 advertised themselves as "ozone-friendly," "biodegradable," "recyclable," "compostable," or something similar—claims that half of all Americans recognize as pure "gimmickry." Environmentalists in the Netherlands and France have attempted to cut away such misinformation by introducing a 12-point environmental advertising code through their national legislatures. Ten state attorneys general are pushing for similar national standards in the United States. Meanwhile, official and unofficial organizations throughout Europe, North America, and Japan have initiated "green labeling" programs, aiming to steer consumers to environmentally preferable products.[16]

The rise of green consumerism is a hopeful sign. As shoppers bring environmental considerations into stores, consumer product companies have little choice but to take ecology more seriously than in the past. To date, most have taken it far more seriously in marketing than in manufacturing, but incremental progress is evident. McDonald's and Procter & Gamble are two major corporations that have somewhat reduced their use of packaging as a result of consumer pressure. At its best, green consumerism is a potent new tactic for environmental advocates, allowing them to bypass the halls of parliaments and send their message directly to boardrooms. At its worst, green consumerism is a palliative for the conscience of the consumer class, allowing us to continue business as usual while feeling like we are doing our part.[17]

Efforts to restrict advertising of tobacco and alcohol, to curtail advertising to children, and to regulate environmental claims of marketers are parts of a broader agenda. The nonprofit Center for the Study of Commercialism in Washington, D.C., is calling for an end to brand name plugs in feature films, for schools to declare themselves advertising-free zones, and for revision of the tax code so that money spent on advertising is taxable.[18]

Television, besides carrying many of the commercial messages, reinforces consumerist values. It is a fixture of life in the consumer society. Almost every household has a set—or two or three—and those sets are on much of the day, seven hours a day in the United States, issuing a stream of soap operas, situation comedies, music videos, and sales spiels. Aside from sleeping and working, watching television is the leading activity in most consumer societies, from the United States and the United Kingdom to Japan and Singapore.[19]

All that television time would not be worrisome for the environment were it not for the message of most programming, because the technology itself—like most communications media—uses comparatively little energy and materials. The messages are the problem: commercial television promotes the restless craving for more by portraying the high consumption life-style as a model to be emulated.

Commercial TV is advancing around the world, and everywhere it has proved exceptionally effective at stimulating buying urges. As Anthony J.F. Reilly, chief executive of the food conglomerate H.J. Heinz, told *Fortune* magazine, "Once television is there, people of whatever shade, culture, or origin want roughly the same things." Harnessed as an educational tool, TV can be powerful, as in India and Africa, where lessons are beamed to teacher-less villages. But the overwhelming trend in broadcasting almost everywhere is commercialization. In 1985, the International Advertising Association rhapsodized: "The magical marketing tool of television has been bound with the chains of laws and regulations, in much of the world, and it has not been free to exercise more than a tiny fraction of its potential as a conduit of the consumer information and economic stimulation provided by advertising. Those chains are at last being chiseled off."[20]

During the eighties, governments deregulated or privatized television programming in most of Western Europe. Public broadcasting monopolies splintered in Belgium, France, Italy, Germany, Norway, Portugal, Spain, and Switzerland—allowing advertising on a scale previously witnessed only in the United States. As the European Community becomes both a single market and a common broadcasting region starting in 1993, European TV time will become a bonanza, with its access to the region's 330 million consumers and $4 trillion of disposable income.[21]

And commercial television is quickly spreading beyond the consumer class. In India, declares Gurcharan Das, chairman of Procter & Gamble India, "an advertiser can reach 200 million people every night" through television. India has gone from 3 million TVs in

1983 to more than 14 million today. Latin America has built or imported 60 million sets, almost one per family, since the early fifties. All told, perhaps half the world's people have ready access to televisions.[22]

For many of the poor around the world, what appears to be the land of milk and honey—the West—is visible nightly on the world's 800 million television sets. Quechua-speaking Indian communities on the Bolivian altiplano use portable satellite dishes to tune in "Miami Vice" and Brazilian soap operas. Herders on the Mongolian steppes retune their antennas away from official government broadcasts to watch commercial-packed music videos beamed by satellite from Hong Kong. Australian aborigines in the outback pick up "Dallas." Former advertising executive and media critic Jerry Mander estimates that half the programs aired outside the United States are American reruns. More broadly, the American entertainment industry, including motion pictures, music, and videos along with television programming, is the nation's second biggest export earner. Partly as a consequence, aspirations everywhere are defined by the current norm in the United States.[23]

One risk of commercial television is that it homogenizes human cultures, leading to a loss of healthy diversity and to a weakening of attachments to local places. "As the world becomes 'smaller,' " reports one consulting firm, surveying emerging Third World markets, "there is greater worldwide uniformity in consumer tastes." Cindy Gilday, a native American woman of the Dene tribe in Canada's Northwest Territory, describes the arrival of television in her community: "When TV came to the villages, I saw an immediate change. People lost interest in the native stories, legends, and languages, which are really important because they teach people how to live. We used to honor our old people and listen to them, but that's changing fast." She notes that "our traditions have a lot to do with survival. Cooperation, sharing, and nonmaterialism are the only ways that people can live here. TV always seems to present values opposite to those."[24]

Television also appears to cut into time people spend in conversation. In the United States, watching television is among the fastest-growing uses of time (shopping is another growing category), while time spent in conversation with friends and family has declined. Perhaps, for the consumer class, the television plays the role that the hearth played in dwellings of yesteryear—something captivating to watch and draw the family together. Of course, fires do not advertise, nor stifle conversation. (Interestingly, in one survey, Americans ranked watching television their seventeenth favorite on a list of 22 daily activities, beneath many things they spend far less time doing, such as reading.)[25]

Just as the expanding reach of advertising is not going unchallenged, small networks of citizens everywhere are beginning to confront commercial television. In Vancouver, British Columbia, English teacher Michael Maser gets secondary students to study television production so they will be able to recognize techniques used to manipulate viewers' sentiments. Millions of young people could benefit from such a course, considering how many products are pitched at them on TV. American children and teenagers sit through about three hours of television commercials each week—20,000 ads a year, 360,000 by the time they graduate from secondary school. Since 1989, the Center for Media and Values in Los Angeles has been promoting media literacy, along the lines taught by Maser, by furnishing parents throughout North America with tips on teaching their children to watch with a critical eye.[26]

More boldly, some attempt to storm the battlements of commercial television itself. Dianne Grenier rallied the town of Andover, Connecticut, to join her in a week's moratorium on watching television. "No TV" week was a great success. Community events were well attended, bringing neighbors together as rarely before, and couples reported both that they were talking more between themselves and that their children were playing more creatively.[27]

Commercial television needs fundamental reorientation if consumerist values are to shift sufficiently to sustain the earth. The Vancouver-based Media Foundation is building a movement aimed at turning television to nonconsuming ends. Local groups raise funds to air the group's spots on commercial television. By the end of 1991, the spots had run in California, Ontario, and a half-dozen other states and provinces. Their "Tube Head" series of paid advertisements tell viewers to shut off the set. The premier spot in their "High on the Hog" campaign shows a gigantic animated pig frolicking on a map of North America while a narrator intones: "Five percent of the people in the world consume *one-third* of the planet's resources. . . . Those people are us." The pig belches.[28]

The spread of commercial television and advertising are two important forces that cultivate needs. The commercialization of public spaces is a third. Shopping malls are taking over many of the functions of public spaces, including both commerce and recreation. Mall planners testify to the importance that customers place on feeling a sense of community where they shop by designing the complexes as imitation communities.

Malls present themselves as safe, prosperous, and tidy neighborhoods where cordial shopkeepers care for their patrons and quiet fountains relax weary minds. Yet the community of the mall is illusory: the omnipresence of sales in retail complexes subtly shifts the emphasis from being to buying.[29]

The United States provides the extreme case of mall development. The almost 35,000 shopping centers there surpassed high schools in number in 1987. Over the past three decades, shopping center space has grown twelvefold; 2,000 new centers opened each year from 1986 to 1989. With so many malls to choose from, centers that want to stand out go to great lengths to attract customers. Among the most successful is Potomac Mills. A huge expanse of glass and concrete in the countryside of rural Virginia, Potomac Mills boasts enough discount retail outlets to draw crowds from great distances. Bus tours from as far away as Connecticut helped bring the number of patrons to 12 million in 1990, making Potomac Mills Mall the leading tourist attraction in Virginia.[30]

Potomac Mills will likely soon be eclipsed, however, by the Mall of America, which opened in Bloomington, Minnesota, in June 1992—the largest shopping center in the world. Along with four department stores and 400 specialty shops, the center offers patrons a three-hectare Camp Snoopy theme park, a giant walk-through aquarium, a two-story miniature golf course, countless cinemas and restaurants, plus some 13,000 parking spaces. Shopping centers such as these, along with thousands of more modest ones throughout the United States, now garner 55 percent of retail sales nationwide, compared with 16 percent in France and 4 percent in Spain.[31]

Suburban malls and commercial strips suck com-

merce away from downtown and neighborhood merchants. In Denver, Colorado, each of six suburban malls
takes in more dollars from sales than does the downtown
commercial district. Shopping by public transit or on
foot becomes difficult, auto traffic increases, and sprawl
accelerates. In the end, noncommercial public places
such as town squares and city streets are robbed of their
vitality, leaving us fewer attractive places to go besides
the malls that set the whole process in motion.[32]

Perhaps by default, malls have taken over some of the
traditional functions of public spaces. They offer entertainment in the forms of video arcades and multiscreen
theaters, and exercise centers of all types. Avia, a leading
sports footwear manufacturer, has even introduced a
shoe especially designed for mall walking. William
Kowinski writes in *The Malling of America*: "Someday it
may be possible to be born, go from preschool through
college, get a job, date, marry, have children . . . get a
divorce, advance through a career or two, receive your
medical care, even get arrested, tried, and jailed; live a
relatively full life of culture and entertainment, and
eventually die and be given funeral rites without ever
leaving a particular mall complex—because every one of
those possibilities exists now in some shopping center
somewhere."[33]

Particularly in the United States, shopping has
become a primary cultural activity. Americans go to
shopping centers on average once a week—more often
than they go to church or synagogue. They spend six
hours a week doing various types of shopping—more
than even Russians did in the late eighties, when Soviet
shopping queues were world-famous. American teenagers spend more time in malls than anywhere besides
school or home. The time Americans spend shopping is

second only to that spent watching television when it comes to categories of time use that have grown fastest since mid-century.[34]

The consumer society makes shopping an especially important role for females. Some 93 percent of American teenage girls surveyed in 1987 deemed shopping their favorite pastime. Toy manufacturers cash in handsomely on the shopping passions of young girls. A Mattel advertisement from England is typical, showing a four-year-old girl smiling ebulliently beside the toy shopping cart she has stacked full of household goods. The copy exclaims, "The house can become a shopping mall. And every room a store, bursting with fascinating things to buy. All it takes is a preschooler's imagination. And the Tuff Stuff Shoppin' Basket." Karen Christensen, a student of the home economy, believes that shopping plays a special role for women who do not work outside of the home. It is the rare domestic responsibility that puts them in contact with other adults—and in public places where they feel both welcomed and safe.[35]

Yet a mall is not a community. It is a commercial enterprise, designed in minute detail to prompt impulse buying. It artificially isolates people from the cycles of nature, from the time of day, and from changes of weather. It excludes those who cannot afford to spend on a par with the rest of the consumer class. And rather than grounding people in attachments to their neighbors and their place, it fosters a sort of care-free anonymity.

Although no country rivals the United States in shopping malls, centers are sprouting across the landscape in many nations. Spain's 90-odd centers are expected to triple in number by early 1993. Mall development is booming in Mexico and "sizzling" in Puerto Rico, according to industry analysts. Britain's bevy of one-stop superstores doubled to about 500 during the eighties, and floor space in British shopping centers jumped tenfold between 1986 and 1990. Italy, despite its strong tradition of community merchants, has recently relaxed controls on mall development, leading to predictions that its shopping centers will multiply from 35 to 100 in five years. Even in France, where the passion for fresh foods is legend, the microwave and the *grande surface* (shopping mall) are edging out bakeries, dairies, and farmers' markets.[36]

Among industrial countries, Japan has been the biggest standout against shopping mall development. Commerce there remains dominated by thousands of local "mom-and-pop" stores woven through Japan's urban fabric. Much shopping continues to take place in neighborhood lanes, which are closed to traffic during certain hours to become *hokoosha tengoku*, literally "pedestrian heavens." The shops, in small buildings that are also homes for the merchants, have relatively high prices, but also allow the Japanese to do most shopping on foot. The political power of Japan's 1.6 million small-business owners protected this pattern of commerce over decades—tying up most large retail development plans in the red tape of the locally controlled zoning process. Yet in the late eighties, U.S. trade negotiators began exerting intense pressure on the Japanese government to repeal or reform the Large-Scale Retail Store Law that allowed such local participation. The law, they argued, was a secret barrier to international trade, because American manufacturers were unable to steer their wares through the winding channels of the traditional distribution system that serves such neighborhood shops.[37]

With the relaxation of rules that has followed U.S. pressure, traditional vegetable stands and fish shops in Japan are starting to give way to supermarkets and convenience stores; along the way, styrofoam and plastic film have replaced newspaper as fish wrap. Large retailers from the United States have also opened shop in the nation: Toys "R" Us, Inc. alone plans to open 10 outlets a year, each offering 8,000 distinct, mostly plastic playthings. Developers are now constructing hundreds of large stores and dozens of shopping malls in Japan. The Japan Council of Shopping Centers tallied six malls opening a month in 1991, and expects the total number to double by 2000. To compete with the tradition of shopping close to home, the country's new malls build Ferris wheels, churches, pinball parlors, art galleries, fancy tearooms, and, in one case, an indoor ski slope.[38]

Still, in Japan as elsewhere, small merchants and community groups have organized against the incursion of shopping centers. Sixty grassroots groups in Kyoto, Japan, are fighting commercial developments that threaten the small-shops-and-homes character of the city. Antiurban growth activists across the United States have at least slowed the malling of the country. In Massachusetts, architects and urban planners Elizabeth Plater-Zyberk and Andres Duany are not just holding back malls, they are replacing an old mall with a small town. Where there were once hectares of parking lots, there are now narrow lanes with wide sidewalks, a diverse blend of housing and shops, plus a church and library—all designed to get people out of their cars and into community life. Plater-Zyberg dreams of replicating this achievement across the country: "We think of malls as the main focus for retrofitting the suburbs."[39]

Some countries have resisted the advancing shopping

culture, though only rarely is the motivation opposition to consumerism itself. England and Wales have restricted trading on Sundays for 400 years, and labor groups beat back the most recent proposal to lift those limits. Similarly, the protected green belts around British cities have slowed the pace of development of suburban malls there. In Germany, as in much of Europe, stores must close most evenings at 6:00 p.m., and they have limited weekend hours as well. Whatever the motive, these things help control the consumerist influence of marketing on the shape and spirit of public space. Shopping is less likely to become an end in itself if it takes place in stores thoroughly knit into the fabric of the community rather than in massive, insular agglomerations of retail outlets each planned in minute detail to stimulate spendthrift ways. The design of communities shapes human culture.[40]

The forces that manufacture desires—advertising, commercial television, and shopping centers—are so familiar as to go virtually unnoticed in the consumer society, and among the middle-income class they are rapidly becoming pervasive as well. Yet the conscious and widespread cultivation of needs is a relatively recent phenomenon in human history, tracing its roots back scarcely a century. There is no reason these forces cannot be fundamentally redirected—constraining advertising to its appropriate role of informing buyers, turning television to conserving ends, and replacing shopping malls with real communities. Indeed, there is every reason to do so, for the sake of the planet and our own peace of mind.

# 10

# A Culture of Permanence

When Moses came down from Mount Sinai, he could count the rules of ethical behavior on the fingers of his two hands. In the complex global economy of the late twentieth century, in which the simple act of starting an automobile imperceptibly changes the global climate, the rules for ecologically sound living run into the hundreds. But the basic value of a sustainable society, the ecological equivalent of the Golden Rule, is simple: each generation should meet its needs without jeopardizing the prospects for future generations to meet their own needs.[1]

Put into practice, that elementary-sounding principle translates into radical changes. It implies, for example, that we consumers have an ethical obligation to curb our consumption, since it jeopardizes the chances for future generations. Unless we climb down the consumption ladder a few rungs, our grandchildren will inherit a planetary home impoverished by our affluence—a planet whose climate has been drastically altered in mere decades, whose air and water are poisoned, whose fertile soils are worn down, whose living species are decimated in number, and whose wild habitats are shrunken and fragmentary.

Furthermore, unless we lower our consumption we will have no authority to object to the world's present middle-income and poor classes despoiling the earth. A recent cartoon captured the absurdity of the profligate preaching conservation to the poor: the driver of a luxury car idles his gas-guzzling motor and yells to a hungry peasant who is preparing to fell a tree, "Yo! Amigo!! We need that tree to protect us from the greenhouse effect!"[2]

Ultimately, the linked fates of humanity and the natural realm depend on us, the consumers. We can curtail our use of those things that are ecologically destructive, such as fossil fuels, minerals, and paper. And we can cultivate the deeper, nonmaterial sources of fulfillment that are the main psychological determinants of happiness: family and social relationships, meaningful work, and leisure. Or we can abrogate our responsibilities and let our life-style ruin the earth.

Lowering our consumption need not deprive us of goods and services that really matter. To the contrary, life's most meaningful and pleasant activities are often paragons of environmental virtue. The preponderance of things that people name as their most rewarding pastimes—and, interestingly, the things terminally ill individuals choose to do with their remaining months—are infinitely sustainable. Religious practice, conversation, family and community gatherings, theater, music, dance, literature, sports, poetry, artistic and creative pursuits, education, and appreciation of nature all fit readily into a culture of permanence—a way of life that can endure through countless generations.[3]

The first step of reform is uncomplicated. It is to inform consumers of the damage we are causing and how we can avoid it. New values never arrive in the abstract. They come entangled in concrete situations, new realities, and new understandings of the world. Indeed, ethics exist only in practice, in the fine grain of everyday decisions. As Aristotle argued, "In ethics, the decision lies with perception." When most people see a large automobile and think first of the air pollution it causes rather than the social status it conveys, environmental ethics will have arrived. Likewise, when most people see excess packaging, throwaway products, or a new shopping mall and grow angry because they consider them to be crimes against their grandchildren, consumerism will be on the retreat.[4]

Sidney Quarrier, the Connecticut geographer who spent Earth Day 1990 auditing his consumption, demonstrates how information can spur change. Sid still lives far from his job, but he takes the bus to work. Now that his children have grown up and left home, he lives in a smaller house, which he has insulated and weatherized to exceptional levels of energy efficiency. He recycles meticulously, writes letters on the back of scrap paper, and conserves water wherever he can. Sid still wonders "Will the world survive us?" and worries about the driving he does to pursue his passion for photography, but he has become an example to those around him that the culture of permanence can be built one household at a time.[5]

Informing the consumer class is a mammoth task, and in a sense is the overarching goal of most environmental organizations. Since 1989, it has vaulted ahead as literally dozens of authors, publishers, editors, and video producers have brought out guides to personal action for the earth. These volumes, packed with detailed suggestions, have spread quickly. *50 Simple Things You Can Do to Save the Earth* has sold 3.5 million copies in the United States and *The Green Consumer* was a best seller in the United Kingdom. Sometimes criticized for personalizing systemic problems, these guides nonetheless provide information most members of the consumer society had previously lacked about practical ways to slow the waste of the earth.[6]

Personal efforts to live more gently on the earth reach their logical conclusion in the quest for simpler living more generally. The attempt to live by nonmaterialistic definitions of success is not new, of course. Researcher Duane Elgin estimated in 1981—perhaps optimistically—that 10 million adult Americans were experimenting "wholeheartedly" with voluntary simplicity. Germany, India, the Netherlands, Norway, the United Kingdom, and many other nations all have small segments of their populations who try to adhere to a nonconsuming philosophy.[7]

For these practitioners, the goal is not ascetic self-denial, but a sort of unadorned grace. Some come to feel, for example, that clotheslines, window shades, and bicycles have a functional elegance that clothes dryers, air conditioners, and automobiles lack. These modest devices are silent, manually operated, fire-proof, ozone- and climate-friendly, easily repaired, and inexpensive. Because they are less "convenient," they breed a degree of forethought and attention to the weather that grounds life in place and time. Karen Christensen, author of *Home Ecology*, emphasizes that living simply need not be drab or tedious: "Instead of consuming things we should cherish and value them. Instead of accepting the sobriquet 'consumer,' we should become not only conservers but creators."[8]

The closest thing to an organized campaign for voluntary simplicity was started by Joe Dominguez, who made a fortune on Wall Street before realizing that getting rich was not making him one whit happier. Today, he lives contentedly on about $500 a month (which, interestingly, puts him in the earnings range of the global middle-income class), and runs the New Road Map Foundation of Seattle, Washington, which he started to disseminate the course he developed on what money can and cannot do. These seminars have helped tens of thousands of people stop fixating on money and start finding out what really makes them happy. They then draw themselves "new road maps" for the future based on their core values. These plans typically reduce graduates' annual spending by 20 percent almost immediately, and allow them to live eventually on much less than they ever thought possible. Many "retire" from earning an income in a matter of years, and dedicate themselves to developing their talents and struggling for causes they hold dear.[9]

Most of the people who come to low consumption, of course, find their way there on their own, not through anything like New Road Map courses. However they get there, enjoying time instead of "spending" it seems central to their values. In 1986, Wanda Urbanska and Frank Levering left their high-paced jobs as journalists and screenwriters in southern California to run the Levering family orchard in rural Virginia. "For us," they

write, "simple living has come to mean spending more
time attending to our lives and less time attending to our
work; devoting less time to earning more money and
more time to the daily doings of life." They live more
deliberately, less hurriedly. " 'Time out,' we've declared. Time out to write letters. Time out to sit on the
porch watching the sun go down, enjoying time. Time
to visit . . . at midmorning or linger with the newspaper
after lunch. To cook from scratch, to tend our two wood
stoves, to make our beds in the mornings and clean our
house on Saturdays."10

Joanne Forman of Taos, New Mexico, agrees that
time is too precious to fritter away on rote consumption:
"I am one of those who voluntarily lives simply, not
because I'm so virtuous, but because I am a composer
and writer, and it comes with the territory; also I hate
housework and am a maniacal reader and hiker. Gradually, I'm having some success with persons like the
friend who is making $250 a month car payments, and
sighs, 'I wish I had time to read.' I point out that she is
working 50 hours a month—more than a week every
month—to pay for her car. This is 'convenience'?"11

Voluntary simplicity as practiced by Dominguez, by
Levering and Urbanska, and by Forman is an ideal. And
for most of us in the consumer class, it may be an unat-
tainable one. Our choices are constrained by the social
pressures, physical infrastructure, and institutional
channels that envelop us. We feel cruel refusing to buy
our children toys that their playmates all have. We
would immobilize ourselves if we abandoned our cars
while still living amidst mass-transit-less, antipedestrian
sprawl. We do not have the option of trading extra salary
for reduced working hours because our employers do
not offer it, and we could not accept it quickly anyway.

Mortgage and car payments, insurance premiums, college tuition, utility bills—we spend most of our disposable income on big-ticket items where the monthly outlay is determined for long stretches at a time. Thus a strategy for reducing consumption must focus as much on changing the framework in which people make choices as it does on the choices they make.

The history of voluntary simplicity movements, furthermore, is not encouraging. As David Shi of North Carolina's Davidson College chronicles, the call for a simpler life has been perennial throughout the history of North America, from the Puritans of Massachusetts Bay to the back-to-the-landers of 20 years ago. None of these movements ever gained more than a slim minority of adherents. And while simplicity fads have swept the continent periodically, most have ended in consumption binges that more than made up for past atonement.[12]

Elsewhere, entire nations such as China, Kampuchea, and Vietnam have dedicated themselves to rebuilding human character in a less self-centered mold—sometimes through brutal techniques—but nowhere have they succeeded with more than a token few of their citizens. Most recently, in 1991 Cuba issued bicycles and water buffalo to its workers and farmers in a desperate attempt to survive without Soviet oil or aid. This attempt to impose frugality from on high will likely fare no better than those before it.[13]

On the other hand, potent as the allure of the consumer life-style is, it is not invulnerable. For one thing, consumerism has shallow historical roots. For members of the consumer class, to reject consumerism is not to jettison anything of lasting significance from their cultural inheritance. On the contrary, it is to reaffirm their cultures' most ancient teachings. From a historical perspective, consumerism—not moderation—is the aberrant value system. The consumer life-style is a radical departure from the conserving orientation that human cultures developed over centuries. One way or the other—either because we choose to abandon it, or because it devours its own ecological supports—consumerism is likely to be a short-lived value system as well.

The philosophy of sufficiency, by contrast, is deeply rooted in the human past. Materialism was denounced by all the sages, from Buddha to Muhammad, and every world religion is rife with warnings against the evils of excess. (See Table 10-1.) "These religious founders," observed historian Arnold Toynbee, "disagreed with each other in the pictures of what is the nature of the universe, the nature of the spiritual life, the nature of ultimate reality. But they all agreed in their ethical precepts. . . . They all said with one voice that if we made material wealth our paramount aim, this would lead to disaster."[14]

The revulsion against materialism is as strong in the teachings of the West, where the consumer society eventually took shape, as it is in the East, characterized as "other-worldly" in the western imagination. Indeed, the first western philosopher whose words survive to the present, Thales of Miletus, said 26 centuries ago, "If there is neither excessive wealth nor immoderate poverty in a nation, then justice may be said to prevail."[15]

The Bible—especially important because a majority of the world's consumer class is Christian—echoes most of human wisdom when it asks, "What shall it profit a man if he shall gain the whole world and lose his own soul?" Saint Francis of Assisi, Saint Thomas Aquinas, Saint Augustine, and church leaders through the ages have all held immoderate wealth a sin, and from ancient

TABLE 10-1. *Teachings of World Religions and Major Cultures on Consumption*

| Religion or Culture | Teaching and Source |
| --- | --- |
| American Indian | "Miserable as we seem in thy eyes, we consider ourselves . . . much happier than thou, in this that we are very content with the little that we have." (Micmac chief) |
| Buddhist | "Whoever in this world overcomes his selfish cravings, his sorrows fall away from him, like drops of water from a lotus flower." (*Dhammapada*, 336) |
| Christian | It is "easier for a camel to go through the eye of a needle than for a rich man to enter into the kingdom of God." (*Matthew* 19:23–24) |
| Confucian | "Excess and deficiency are equally at fault." (Confucius, XI.15) |
| Ancient Greek | "Nothing in Excess." (Inscribed at Oracle of Delphi) |
| Hindu | "That person who lives completely free from desires, without longing . . . attains peace." (*Bhagavad-Gita*, II.71) |
| Islamic | "Poverty is my pride." (Muhammad) |
| Jewish | "Give me neither poverty nor riches." (*Proverbs* 30:8) |
| Taoist | "He who knows he has enough is rich." (*Tao Te Ching*) |

SOURCES: Compiled by Worldwatch Institute.

to Medieval times, monks under their vows of poverty held higher social rank than successful merchants.[16]

Less vaunted sources of wisdom counsel with equal unanimity against the incessant craving for more. In one folk tale from Poland, a fisherman who lives in a hovel by the sea catches a magic fish that grants his humble desire for a cabin and enough to eat. After a week, he is no longer satisfied and returns to the sea to catch the fish again and demand larger quarters, which again are granted. The sequence repeats itself for weeks until he lives in a castle and demands a palace. For his insolence, the fish sends him back to the hovel by the sea. In the same vein, the Roman poet Ovid's tale of the Greek King Midas is told to children throughout the West. Midas was so greedy that he wished he could turn things to gold just by touching them. To his delight, his wish came true, and he proceeded to gild everything in sight. His fate in the end was tragic, though: he killed his own beloved daughter with his magical touch.[17]

Even in the United States, now arguably the most wasteful society in human history, thrift and frugality are the buried touchstones of the national character. None other than Benjamin Franklin wrote, "Money never made a man happy, yet nor will it. There is nothing in its nature to produce happiness. The more a man has, the more he wants. Instead of filling a vacuum, it makes one." Only in this century did consuming rather than saving gain acceptance as a way to live. In 1907, economist Simon Nelson Patten was still considered a heretic when he declared, "The new morality does not consist in saving but in expanding consumption."[18]

Consumerism's roots may be shallow, and it may therefore be vulnerable, but individual action and voluntary simplicity do not appear capable of uprooting it. What must we do, then, to dig it up? The answer may lie in combining the political and the personal. To rejuvenate the ethic of sufficiency, a critical mass of individuals committed to living by it must emerge. But if they are to succeed, they must balance their efforts to change themselves with a bold agenda to challenge the laws, institutions, and interests that profit from profligacy.

Values, after all, are social creations as much as individual ones, and they effectively restrain and direct our behavior only when they are backed up by the force of social institutions. Propagating lower consumption as an ethical norm ultimately requires that we revive the nonconsuming philosophy that lies dormant in our culture—our collective memory, wisdom, and ways—and use it to mold a new culture of permanence.

A culture of permanence will not come quickly. We can expect no instant revolutions in social values, no moral awakening or "paradigm shift." All we can realistically hope for is painfully slow progress against consumerism, punctuated by rapid advances. The stories of cigarettes and ivory illustrate how consumption patterns change as information spreads and personal and political pressure mounts.

For four decades, U.S. health authorities and citizen advocates have warned against smoking, and accumulating scientific evidence has made their case incontrovertible. It was only in the eighties, however, that their efforts finally overcame the social cachet of cigarettes in the United States and the political clout of the tobacco lobby, and they achieved rapid legal advances against smoking. Cigarette consumption there has fallen by a third since 1980.[19]

In the case of ivory, change came more swiftly. Wildlife biologists and conservationists issued repeated pleas during the eighties for an end to the ivory poaching that was exterminating African elephants. The message spread slowly at first, slightly dulling the luster of ivory among the consumer class in North American and

Europe. Late in the decade, the movement's momentum began to build, and in a matter of months in 1989 ivory became taboo for much of the global consumer society. By January 1990, public outcry had turned the informal boycott into a ban on ivory trade and backed it up with the force of international law. As with cigarettes, change came almost imperceptibly for years, before accelerating suddenly to a breakthrough.[20]

Given plenty of time and pressure, conspicuous consumption of all types might decline as have smoking in the United States and ivory sales worldwide. The trouble is, time is awasting for the planet, and constraining consumption of entire categories of products—fossil fuels, for example, or chemicals—is not as simple as doing it for a particular item. The challenge, then, is to generate unprecedented, organized pressure for change, and to aim that pressure where it will have the greatest effect.

Strategic targets clearly include the kinds of laws and policies described in Chapter 8 that favor consumption over leisure, and high-impact commodities over low-impact ones—cars over buses, for instance, or disposables over durables. They also include the excesses of advertising and retailing described in Chapter 9. The contest will be one-sided, for example, so long as commercial television is the dominant cultural force in the consumer society. As religious historian Robert Bellah wrote, "That happiness is to be attained through limitless material acquisition is denied by every religion and philosophy known to humankind, but is preached incessantly by every American television set." And, of course, the wasteful consumer-society approaches to providing food, transport, and materials described in Part II are excellent points to apply pressure.[21]

The best targets are the parts of our consumption that are wasted or unwanted in the first place. Germans drive 6,200 kilometers a year, mostly going places they would not need to drive to if livable neighborhoods were closer to work, a variety of local merchants closer to home, and public transit easier and faster. The Dutch would rather never see most of the 78 kilograms of packaging they have to carry out with the trash each year. Americans feel the same way about the 37 percent of the mail they receive that consists of unsolicited sales pitches. Each day, the United States turns over 23 square kilometers of rural land to new housing developments, "industrial parks," and commercial strips that would mostly be unnecessary if Americans insisted on well-planned land use inside city limits.[22]

Despite the ominous scale of the challenge, there could be many more people ready to begin saying "enough" than prevailing opinion suggests. Polls in the core nations of the consumer society now show that more than half the people prefer protecting the environment if a choice must be made between environmental quality and economic growth. And, thankfully, the consumerist splurge of the eighties is over—although it was halted more by hard times than by concern for the earth. For whatever reasons, as of early 1992, public opinion in at least the United States had swung against crass materialism. The annual surveys of young Americans entering university that have showed material desires soaring since the mid-seventies began after 1987 to show slower growth and even leveling desires for certain consumer goods. And some trend watchers are starting to talk of a sea change in the making. Watts Wacker, vice president of Yankelovich Clancy Shulman, a firm that monitors consumer attitudes, says, "We're moving away from shop-till-you-drop and moving toward dropping shopping.''[23]

In early 1992, little signs of simplifying were everywhere: American fabric stores were experiencing a revival, as more people sewed their own garments. Amy Dacyczyn of Leeds, Maine, calling herself the Frugal Zealot, started a newsletter called the *Tightwad Gazette*, which after two years and no promotional budget already had 50,000 subscribers. Of course, these trends might simply mark another rotation in the binge-and-purge cycle that moral fashion follows as the economy booms and busts, but even so they would represent an opportunity to advance the transition to a culture of permanence.[24]

The future of life on earth depends on whether we among the richest fifth of the world's people, having fully met our material needs, can turn to nonmaterial sources of fulfillment. Whether we—who have defined the tangible goals of world development—can now craft a new way of life at once simpler and more satisfying. Having invented the automobile and airplane, can we return to bicycles, buses, and trains? Having pioneered sprawl and malls, can we recreate human-scale settlements where commerce is an adjunct to civic life rather than its purpose? Having introduced the high fat, junk-food diet, can we instead nourish ourselves on wholesome fare that is locally produced? Having devised disposable plastics, packaging without end, and instantaneous obsolescence, can we design objects that endure and a materials economy that takes care of things?

If our grandchildren are to inherit a planet as bounteous and beautiful as we have enjoyed, we in the consumer class must—without surrendering the quest for advanced, clean technology—eat, travel, and use energy and materials more like those on the middle rung of the world's economic ladder. If we can learn to do so, we might find ourselves happier as well, for in the consumer society, affluence has brought us to a strange pass. Who would have predicted a century ago that the richest civilizations in history would be made up of polluted tracts of suburban development dominated by the private automobile, shopping malls, and a throwaway economy? Surely, this is not the ultimate fulfillment of our destiny.

In the final analysis, accepting and living by sufficiency rather than excess offers a return to what is, culturally speaking, the human home: to the ancient order of family, community, good work, and good life; to a reverence for skill, creativity, and creation; to a daily cadence slow enough to let us watch the sunset and stroll by the water's edge; to communities worth spending a lifetime in; and to local places pregnant with the memories of generations. Perhaps Henry David Thoreau had it right when he scribbled in his notebook beside Walden Pond, "A man is rich in proportion to the things he can afford to let alone."[25]

# For Further Reading
# and Action

For detailed discussions of the various threats to the global environment and their human causes and consequences, see Worldwatch Institute's *State of the World*, published at the beginning of each year, plus the periodic *Worldwatch Papers* (all available for $25 a year from Worldwatch Institute, 1776 Massachusetts Avenue, N.W., Washington, D.C. 20036-1904, (202) 452-1999) and the bimonthly magazine *World Watch* (available for $15 a year from P.O. Box 6991, Syracuse, N.Y. 13217-9942, (800) 825-0061).

Among the dozens of guides on personal action for the environment, *Home Ecology* by Karen Christensen (Golden, Colo.: Fulcrum Publishing, 1990) stands out for its humor and commonsense critique of consumerism. The best-selling *50 Simple Things You Can Do to Save the Earth* is published by the EarthWorks Group (1400 Shattuck Avenue, Box 25,

Berkeley, Calif. 94709). An alternative is the *Ecoteam Workbook*, a complete environmental life-style audit for groups of families (Global Action Plan for the Earth, 449A Route 28A, West Hurley, N.Y. 12491). The New Road Map Foundation's workbook on money, life-style, and values offers an introduction to voluntary simplicity (P.O. Box 15981, Dept. T., Seattle, Wash. 98115). *Tightwad Gazette* (Rural Route 1, Box 3570, Leeds, Maine 04263) provides down-home hints on frugal living.

*In Context* magazine (P.O. Box 11470, Bainbridge Island, Wash. 98110) ran an article called "50 simple things you can do instead of shopping," in their "What's Enough?" edition (Fall 1990). The entire issue is highly recommended. New Ways to Work (149 Ninth Street, San Francisco, Calif. 94103, (415) 552-1000) offers publications on how to shape a meaningful work life without selling short personal life—and suggests strategies for getting employers to allow flexible and reduced schedules.

Moving from the personal to the political, the Media Foundation takes on commercial television and advertising. Get involved through its lively journal *Adbusters Quarterly* (1243 West 7th Ave., Vancouver, B.C., V6H 1B7 Canada, (604) 736-9401). The Center for the Study of Commercialism (1875 Connecticut Ave., N.W., Washington, D.C. 20009-5728) points a spotlight at egregious instances of commercialism. The Center for Media and Values offers kits to help children develop critical TV viewing skills (1962 S. Shenandoah Street, Los Angeles, Calif. 90034, (213) 202-1936).

For a step into food activism, here are two places to start. The Natural Resources Defense Council is campaigning to end grazing subsidies that accelerate the desertification of the western United States (90 New Montgomery, #620, San Francisco, Calif. 94105). Earthsave informs Americans of the diverse environmental effects of livestock production (P.O. Box 949, Felton, Calif. 95018).

Aspiring transportation reformers might contact three organizations. The National Association of Railroad Passengers (900 2nd Street N.E., Suite 308, Washington D.C. 20002) and Transit NOW (1317 F Street, N.W., Suite 600, Washington, D.C. 20004) are working to promote rail and other forms of energy-efficient transportation. The Institute for Transportation and Development Policy (1787 Columbia Rd., N.W., #300, Washington, D.C. 20009) coordinates bike shipments to developing countries and pushes for humanpowered transportation policies in development plans.

Those concerned with rejuvenating the conserving form of materialism can lend support to three others. Phil Hocker's Minerals Policy Center (1325 Massachusetts Avenue, N.W., Suite 550, Washington, D.C. 20005) is attacking the mining industry head-on by challenging the General Mining Act of 1872, which serves up the nation's public lands on a platter to miners. The Association of Forest Service Employees for Environmental Ethics is fighting a parallel battle for the nation's publicly owned forests, trying to get the agency to put forest ecology ahead of wood output (P.O. Box 11615, Eugene, Oreg. 97440). At the other end of the materials stream, Paul and Ellen Connett's Work on Waste USA Inc. (82 Judson, Canton, N.Y. 13617) builds barricades against the spread of large solid waste incinerators—the latest high-tech, energy-wasting "solution" to material excess.

For those interested in theoretical questions, two volumes look at the psychology of consumption in depth: Paul Wachtel's *The Poverty of Affluence* (Philadelphia: New Society Publishers, 1989) and Tibor Scitovsky's *The Joyless Economy* (New York: Oxford University Press, 1976). Two others examine the environmentally blind economic system that feeds consumption: *Small Is Beautiful: Economics as if People Mattered* by E.F. Schumacher (New York: Harper & Row, 1973) and *For the Common Good: Redirecting the Economy Toward Community, the Environment, and a Sustainable Future* by Herman E. Daly and John B. Cobb, Jr. (Boston: Beacon Press, 1989). On the choice between more stuff and more time, see Juliet Schor, *The Overworked American: The Unexpected Decline of Leisure* (New York: Basic Books, 1992).

For a thorough history of voluntary simplicity movements in North America, see David Shi, *The Simple Life: Plain Living and High Thinking in American Culture* (New York: Oxford University Press, 1985). Among the best looks at the spiritual shortcomings of consumerism is Charlene Spretnak, *States of Grace: The Recovery of Meaning in the Postmodern Age* (San Francisco: HarperCollins Publishers, 1991).

The passionate writings of Wendell Berry stand alone among contemporary writings on environmental values for their lucidity and eloquence. See *The Unsettling of America* (New York: Avon, 1977), *The Gift of Good Land* (San Francisco: North Point Press, 1981), and *Home Economics* (San Francisco: North Point Press, 1987).

Finally, to post at school or the office, Sidney Quarrier's complete 20-year consumption list is reproduced on a clever educational poster, "Something's Got to Give" (from Department of Environmental Protection, 165 Capitol Avenue, Room 555, Hartford, Conn. 06106).

# Notes

CHAPTER 1. The Conundrum of Consumption

1. Sidney Quarrier, geologist, Connecticut Geological & Natural History Survey, Hartford, Conn., private communication, February 25, 1992.
2. Ibid.
3. Ibid.
4. Ibid.
5. Lebow in *Journal of Retailing*, quoted in Vance Packard, *The Waste Makers* (New York: David Mckay, 1960).
6. Sepp Linhart, "From Industrial to Postindustrial Society: Changes in Japanese Leisure-Related Values and Behavior," *Journal of Japanese Studies*, Summer 1988; Richard A. Easterlin and Eileen M. Crimmins, "Recent Social Trends: Changes in Personal Aspirations of American Youth," *Sociology and Social Research*, July 1988; "Dynasty" from "Harper's Index," *Harper's*, December 1990; "Dallas" from Jerry Mander, *In the Absence of the Sacred* (San Francisco: Sierra Club Books, 1991); Taiwan from "Asian Century," *Newsweek*, February 22, 1988; Stephen

Baker and S. Lynne Walker, "The American Dream is Alive and Well—in Mexico," *Business Week*, September 30, 1991.

7. Billionaires from Jennifer Reese, "The Billionaires: More Than Ever in 1991," *Fortune*, September 9, 1991; millionaires estimated from Kevin R. Phillips, "Reagan's America: A Capital Offense," *New York Times Magazine*, June 18, 1990; homelessness from U.N. Centre for Human Settlements, New York, private communication, November 1, 1989; luxury goods from "The Lapse of Luxury," *Economist*, January 5, 1991; gross national product from United Nations Development Programme, *Human Development Report 1991* (New York: Oxford University Press, 1991); member countries in United Nations from U.N. Information Center, Washington, D.C., private communication, January 14, 1992; world average income from 1987, in 1987 U.S. dollars adjusted for international variations in purchasing power, from Ronald V.A. Sprout and James H. Weaver, "International Distribution of Income: 1960-1987," Working Paper No. 159, Department of Economics, American University, Washington, D.C., May 1991; U.S. 1987 poverty line for an individual from U.S. Bureau of the Census, *Statistical Abstract of the United States: 1990* (Washington, D.C.: U.S. Government Printing Office, 1990).

8. Four-and-a-half times richer from Angus Maddison, *The World Economy in the 20th Century* (Paris: Organisation for Economic Co-operation and Development, 1989).

9. Alan Durning, *Poverty and the Environment: Reversing the Downward Spiral*, Worldwatch Paper 92 (Washington, D.C.: Worldwatch Institute, November 1989).

## CHAPTER 2. The Consumer Society

1. Estimated annual earnings per family member, in 1988 U.S. dollars of gross domestic product (GDP) per capita adjusted for international variations in purchasing power, and share of world income from Ronald V.A. Sprout and James H. Weaver, "1988 International Distribution of Income" (unpublished data) provided by Ronald V.A. Sprout, U.N. Economic Commission for Latin America and the Caribbean, Washington Office, Washington, D.C., private communication, January 2, 1992. Sprout and Weaver combined income distribution data and purchasing-power adjusted GDP per capita data to disaggregate 127 countries into five classes each and reaggregate these segments into five global classes; see Ronald V.A. Sprout and James H. Weaver, "International Distribution of Income: 1960-1987," Working

Paper No. 159, Department of Economics, American University, Washington, D.C., May 1991. Number in each class adjusted to mid-year 1992 population from Machiko Yanagishita, demographer, Population Reference Bureau, Washington, D.C., private communication, February 26, 1992.

2. Income range and share of world income estimated from Sprout and Weaver, "1988 International Distribution of Income"; Chinese appliances from "TV Now in 50% of Homes," *China Daily*, February 15, 1988.

3. Income range and share of world income from Sprout and Weaver, "1988 International Distribution of Income"; comparison to U.S. poverty line from U.S. Bureau of the Census, *Statistical Abstract of the United States: 1990* (Washington, D.C.: U.S. Government Printing Office, 1990). As used in this book, "consumers," "consumer class," and "global consumer society" are synonymous and refer to the richest fifth of humanity as measured by per capita income or life-style. The global consumer society, of course, does not share the institutions that a national society does, but it does share a way of life and many values.

4. Sprout and Weaver, "1988 International Distribution of Income." See also Nathan Keyfitz, "Consumerism and the New Poor," *Society*, January/February 1992.

5. Highest paid fifth of Americans from Robert B. Reich, "Secession of the Successful," *New York Times Magazine*, January 20, 1991; pay gap from Robert B. Reich, *The Work of Nations: Preparing Ourselves for 21st Century Capitalism* (New York: Alfred A. Knopf, 1991).

6. Consumption trends are Worldwatch Institute estimates, based on copper and aluminum from United Nations (UN), *Statistical Yearbook, 1953* (New York: 1954), and from UN, *Statistical Yearbook, 1985/86* (New York: 1988); on energy from UN, *World Energy Supplies 1950-1974* (New York: 1976), and from UN, *1987 Energy Statistics Yearbook* (New York: 1989); on meat from UN, *Statistical Yearbook, 1953*, and from Linda M. Bailey, agricultural economist, U.S. Department of Agriculture, Washington, D.C., private communication, September 11, 1990; on steel, wood, cement, and air travel from UN, *Statistical Yearbook, 1953*, and from U.S. Bureau of the Census, *Statistical Abstract of the United States: 1990* (Washington, D.C.: U.S. Government Printing Office, 1990); on car ownership from UN, *Statistical Yearbook, 1953*, and from Motor Vehicle Manufacturers Association (MVMA), *Facts and Figures '90* (Detroit, Mich.: 1990); and on plastic from UN, *Statistical Yearbook, 1970* (New York: 1971), and from UN, *Statistical Yearbook, 1983/84* (New York: 1985).

Throughout this book, population data used to calculate per capita consumption are from UN, *Statistical Yearbook, 1975* (New York: 1975), from UN, *Statistical Yearbook, 1983/84*, and from UN, *Statistical Yearbook, 1985/86*, with two exceptions: recent years from Population Reference Bureau, *Population Data Sheet* (Washington, D.C.: various years), and data for United States from U.S. Bureau of the Census, *Statistical Abstract of the United States: 1979* (Washington, D.C.: U.S. Government Printing Office, 1979), and from Bureau of the Census, *Statistical Abstract of the United States: 1990*.

7. History of consumerism from Stuart Ewen, *Captains of Consciousness* (New York: McGraw-Hill, 1976), from Susan Strasser, *Satisfaction Guaranteed: The Making of the American Mass Market* (New York: Pantheon Books, 1989), and from Benjamin Kline Hunnicutt, *Work Without End: Abandoning Shorter Hours for the Right to Work* (Philadelphia: Temple University Press, 1988); National Prosperity Bureau quoted in David E. Shi, *The Simple Life: Plain Living and High Thinking in American Culture* (New York: Oxford University Press, 1985).

8. *Fortune* quoted in Shi, *Simple Life*; consumer purchases and cost of living index—the Consumer Price Index—from Reich, *The Work of Nations*.

9. Chairman quoted in Reich, *The Work of Nations*; cars from MVMA, *Facts and Figures '90*, and from MVMA, Detroit, Mich., private communication, July 10, 1990; car-miles from U.S. Department of Energy (DOE), Energy Information Administration (EIA), *Annual Energy Review 1988* (Washington, D.C.: 1989), and from Paul Svercl, Federal Highway Administration, Washington, D.C., private communication, August 21, 1990; plastics from Sara Spivey, Society for the Plastics Industry, Washington D.C., private communication, August 23, 1990; air travel from Mary C. Holcomb et al., *Transportation Energy Data Book: Edition 9* (Oak Ridge, Tenn.: Oak Ridge National Laboratory, 1987), and from Federal Aviation Administration, Washington, D.C., private communication, August 17, 1990.

10. Tokyo Disneyland from Yumiko Ono, "Japanese Firms Get Serious About Amusement Parks," *Asian Wall Street Journal*, August 10-11, 1990, and from Priscilla Painton, "Fantasy's Reality," *Time*, May 27, 1991; consumer information, Coca-Cola Company, Atlanta, Ga., private communication, January 21, 1992; "Golden Arches to Be Built With Recyclables," *Biocycle*, May 1990; Singaporean youngsters from Dinah Lee, "Asia: The Next Era of Growth," *Business Week*, November 11, 1991.

11. Steel, cement, aluminum, and paper from Eric Larsen, Center for Energy and Environmental Studies, Princeton University, Princeton, N.J., unpublished data, 1990; frozen foods from Euromonitor Publications Ltd., *Consumer Europe 1985* (London: 1985) and *Consumer Europe 1991* (London: 1991); soft drinks and autos from Euromonitor, *Consumer Europe 1991.*

12. Japan trends in aluminum (from 1960 to 1987) from UN, *Statistical Yearbook, 1961* (New York: 1962), and from UN, *Statistical Yearbook, 1985/86*; energy from UN, *World Energy Supplies, 1950-1974*, and from UN, *1987 Energy Statistics Yearbook*; steel from UN, *Statistical Yearbook, 1953*, and U.S. Bureau of the Census, *Statistical Abstract of the United States: 1990*; cars from UN, *Statistical Yearbook, 1953*, and from MVMA, *Facts and Figures '90*; meat from Bailey, private communication; travel in 1972 from Sepp Linhart, "From Industrial to Postindustrial Society: Changes in Japanese Leisure-Related Values and Behavior," *Journal of Japanese Studies*, Summer 1988; 1990 travel from "Rich Girls with Wanderlust," *Japan Economic Journal*, March 3, 1990.

13. Refrigerators, clothes washers and dryers, and dishwashers from Euromonitor Publications Ltd., *International Marketing Data and Statistics 1986/87* (London: 1988), from Organisation for Economic Co-operation and Development, *State of the Environment, 1991* (Paris: 1991), from Euromonitor Publications Ltd., *European Marketing Data and Statistics 1987/88* (London: 1988), and from Euromonitor, *Consumer Europe 1991*; U.S. air conditioning, microwave, and VCR ownership—and data in Figure 2-1—from Bureau of the Census, *Statistical Abstract of the United States: 1979*, and from DOE, EIA, *Annual Energy Review 1990* (Washington, D.C.: 1991); air conditioning electricity from Edison Electric Institute, cited in Robert J. Samuelson, "The Chilling of America," *Washington Post*, June 6, 1991; Japanese air conditioning from Euromonitor Publications, Ltd., *Consumer Japan 1990* (London: 1990).

14. Trends in eighties from Kevin R. Phillips, "Reagan's America: A Capital Offense," *New York Times Magazine*, June 18, 1990; Jaguars and fur coats from Myron Magnet, "The Money Society," *Fortune*, July 6, 1987; private security from Reich, *The Work of Nations.*

15. "Japan's Baby Boomer's Spending Lavishly in Single Minded Pursuit of the Good Life," *Japan Economic Journal*, April 11, 1990; Yorimoto Katsumi, "Tokyo's Serious Waste Problem," *Japan Quarterly*, July/September 1990; spending and student quote from Fred Hiatt and Margaret Shapiro, "Sudden Riches

Creating Conflict and Self-Doubt," *Washington Post*, February 11, 1990.

16. "Consumerism" is used in this book as a looser term than consumer society, consumer class, or consumer. It refers to the cultural attitude, common among consumers but also found among many lower on the global economic ladder, that attributes great importance to possessing and using a growing number and variety of goods and services. Paul Ekins, "The Sustainable Consumer Society: A Contradiction in Terms?" *International Environmental Affairs*, Fall 1991. Japan polls from Linhart, "From Industrial to Postindustrial Society."

17. 1967 figures cited in Richard A. Easterlin and Eileen M. Crimmins, "Recent Social Trends: Changes in Personal Aspirations of American Youth," *Sociology & Social Research*, July 1988; 1990 figures from Alexander W. Astin et al., *The American Freshman: National Norms for Fall 1990* (Los Angeles: Cooperative Institutional Research Program, University of California, 1990); Cornell student quoted in Blayne Cutler, "Up the Down Staircase," *American Demographics*, April 1989.

18. Eileen M. Crimmins et al., "Preference Changes Among American Youth: Family, Work, and Goods Aspirations, 1976-86," *Population and Development Review*, March 1991, and Richard A. Easterlin and Eileen M. Crimmins, "Private Materialism, Personal Fulfillment, Family Life, and Public Interest: The Nature, Effects, and Causes of Recent Changes in the Values of American Youth," *Public Opinion Quarterly*, Vol. 55, 1991.

19. Share of East Europeans in consumer class estimated from Sprout and Weaver, "1988 International Distribution of Income"; Budapest quote from Timothy Harper, "In Budapest, the Lines are at McDonald's," *Shopping Centers Today*, May 1989; Ramm quote and auto demand from Marc Fisher, "East Germany and the Wheels of Fortune," *Washington Post*, June 3, 1990; East German used car sales from "Danke Schon, Trabbie," *Economist*, January 4, 1992.

20. Dowries in India from Vasanth Kannabiran, Deccan Development Society, Pastapur, Andhra Pradesh, India, private communication, July 19, 1991.

21. Prakash Chandra, "India: Middle-Class Spending," *Third World Week* (Institute for Current World Affairs, Hanover, N.H.), March 2, 1990; Anthony Spaeth, "A Thriving Middle Class Is Changing the Face of India," *Wall Street Journal*, May 19, 1988.

22. Korea from Ford S. Worthy, "A New Mass Market Emerges," *Fortune*, Special Issue, Fall 1990; Indonesia from Michael

Vatikiotis, "The Plastic Escape," *Far Eastern Economic Review*, March 21, 1991; Mexico from Stephen S. Baker and Lynne Walker, "The American Dream is Alive and Well—in Mexico," *Business Week*, September 30, 1991.

CHAPTER 3. The Dubious Rewards of Consumption

1. Aristotle, *Politics*, and Lucretius, *On the Nature of the Universe*, both quoted in Goldian VandenBroeck, ed., *Less Is More: The Art of Voluntary Poverty* (New York: Harper & Row, 1978).
2. Tolstoy, *My Religion*, quoted in VandenBroeck, *Less is More*.
3. Lewis H. Lapham, *Money and Class in America: Notes and Observations on Our Civil Religion* (New York: Weidenfeld & Nicolson, 1988).
4. Worldwatch Institute estimate of consumption since 1950 based on gross world product data from Angus Maddison, *The World Economy in the 20th Century* (Paris: Organisation for Economic Co-operation and Development, 1989); minerals from Ralph C. Kirby and Andrew S. Prokopovitsh, "Technological Insurance Against Shortages in Minerals and Metals," *Science*, February 20, 1976; opinion surveys from Michael Worley, National Opinion Research Center, University of Chicago, Chicago, Ill., private communication, September 19, 1990; gross national product per capita and personal consumption expenditures are adjusted for inflation from U.S. Bureau of the Census, *Statistical Abstract of the United States: 1991* (Washington, D.C.: U.S. Government Printing Office, 1991).
5. International comparison from R.A. Easterlin, "Does Economic Growth Improve the Human Lot? Some Empirical Evidence," cited in Michael Argyle, *The Psychology of Happiness* (New York: Methuen, 1987); quote from ibid. Similar arguments are found in Angus Campbell, *The Sense of Well-being in America: Recent Patterns and Trends* (New York: McGraw-Hill, 1981), in Paul Wachtel, *The Poverty of Affluence* (Philadelphia: New Society Publishers, 1989), and in F.E. Trainer, *Abandon Affluence* (Atlantic Highlands, N.J.: Zed Books, 1985).
6. Argyle, *The Psychology of Happiness*.
7. Brooke Kroeger, "Feeling Poor on $600,000 a Year," *New York Times*, April 26, 1987; dealmaker quoted in Lapham, *Money and Class in America*.
8. Banker quoted in Kroeger, "Feeling Poor on $600,000 a Year"; Veblen quoted in Lapham, *Money and Class in America*.
9. Argyle, *The Psychology of Happiness*; Tibor Scitovsky, *The Joyless Economy* (New York: Oxford University Press, 1976).

10. Intergenerational rise of consumption standards from Eileen M. Crimmins et al., "Preference Changes Among American Youth: Family, Work, and Goods Aspirations, 1976-86," *Population and Development Review*, March 1991; redefining prosperity as poverty from Scitovsky, *The Joyless Economy*.

11. Endlessly shifting standard of decent living from Scitovsky, *The Joyless Economy*; quote from Crimmins et al., "Preference Changes Among American Youth."

12. Argyle, *Psychology of Happiness*.

13. Scitovsky, *The Joyless Economy*.

14. Argyle, *Psychology of Happiness*.

15. Jeremy Seabrook, *What Went Wrong?* (New York: Pantheon Books, 1978).

16. Ibid.

17. Time spent visiting and conversing from John S. Robinson, "How Americans Use Time," *The Futurist*, September/October 1991; time at meals from Scitovsky, *The Joyless Economy*.

18. Crimmins et al., "Preference Changes Among American Youth."

19. U.S. women's housework before 1965 from David P. Ross and Peter J. Usher, *From the Roots Up: Economic Development as if Community Mattered* (Croton-on-Hudson, N.Y.: The Bootstrap Press, 1986), and from Herman E. Daly and John B. Cobb, Jr., *For the Common Good: Redirecting the Economy Toward Community, the Environment, and a Sustainable Future* (Boston: Beacon Press, 1989); women's housework since 1965 from Robinson, "How Americans Use Time"; U.K. housework from Ross and Usher, *From the Roots Up*.

20. U.S. food budget from Leonard L. Berry, "Market to the Perception," *American Demographics*, February 1990; diapers from Blayne Cutler, "Rock-A-Buy Baby," *American Demographics*, January 1990.

21. History from Susan Strasser, *Satisfaction Guaranteed: The Making of the American Mass Market* (New York: Pantheon Books, 1989), from Witold Rybczinski, "Living Smaller," *Atlantic Monthly*, February 1991, and from Nicholas Lemann, "Stressed Out in Suburbia," *Atlantic Monthly*, November 1989; British gardens from Jennifer Foote, "How Does the Garden Grow?" *Newsweek*, July 15, 1991.

22. History from Dolores Hayden, *Redesigning the American Dream: The Future of Housing, Work, and Family Life* (New York: W.W. Norton & Co., 1984); frequency of moving from Robert Reich, "A Question of Geography," *New Republic*, May 9, 1988.

23. Carl Gardner and Julie Shepard, *Consuming Passion: The Rise of Retail Culture* (London: Unwin Hyman, 1990).

24. Robert V. Levine, "The Pace of Life," *American Scientist*, September/October 1990.
25. E. F. Schumacher, *Good Work* (New York: Harper & Row Publishers, 1979); George Watson, "The Decay of Idleness," *Wilson Quarterly*, Spring 1991; leisure wear from Witold Rybczynski, "Waiting for the Weekend," *Atlantic Monthly*, August 1991; Sepp Linhart, "From Industrial to Postindustrial Society: Changes in Japanese Leisure-Related Values and Behavior," *Journal of Japanese Studies*, Summer 1988; Range Rovers from T.R. Reid, "U.S. Automakers Grind Gears in Japan," *Washington Post*, September 23, 1990; "With Permit Rules Relaxed, Log Cabin Sales Are Soaring," *Japan Economic Journal*, August 4, 1990.
26. Rybczynski, "Waiting for the Weekend."

## CHAPTER 4. The Environmental Costs of Consumption

1. *Shorter Oxford Dictionary* quoted in Paul Ekins, "The Sustainable Consumer Society: A Contradiction in Terms?" *International Environmental Affairs*, Fall 1991.
2. Carbon emissions exclude the 7-33 percent that originate from forest clearing. Although this somewhat biases the figures against the consumer class—forest clearing emissions are concentrated in rural areas of developing countries, where many of the poor live—emissions of other greenhouse gases, such as chlorofluorocarbons, are more concentrated in the consumer society than fossil-derived carbon dioxide. Thus, fossil-fuel carbon emissions are a relatively good overall indicator of responsibility for global warming. The estimates of emissions by class assume—plausibly—that carbon emissions and world income distribution coincide, and were calculated by combining income distribution data from World Bank, *World Development Report 1991* (New York: Oxford University Press, 1991), with carbon emissions data from Gregg Marland et al., *Estimates of CO$_2$ Emissions from Fossil Fuel Burning and Cement Manufacturing, Based on the United Nations Energy Statistics and the U.S. Bureau of Mines Cement Manufacturing Data* (Oak Ridge, Tenn.: Oak Ridge National Laboratory, 1989), and from Thomas Boden et al., *Trends '91* (Oak Ridge, Tenn.: Oak Ridge National Laboratory, in press), and comparing them with Ronald V.A. Sprout and James H. Weaver, "1988 International Distribution of Income" (unpublished data) provided by Ronald V.A. Sprout, U.N. Economic Commission for Latin America and the Caribbean, Washington Office, Washington, D.C., private communication, January 2, 1992.
3. Table 4-1 based on U.N. data for 1987-88 reported in Jyoti Pa-

rikh and Kirit Parikh, "Role of Unsustainable Consumption Patterns and Population in Global Environmental Stress," *Sustainable Development* (New Delhi), October 1991, with the exceptions of timber (industrial roundwood) from U.N. Food and Agriculture Organization (FAO), *Forestry Statistics Today for Tomorrow, 1961-89, Wood and Wood Products* (Rome: 1991), of fish from FAO, *Fisheries Statistics Commodities Yearbook 1989* (Rome: 1991), of meat from *Production Yearbook 1989* (Rome: 1990), and of water from World Resources Institute, *World Resources 1990-91* (New York: Oxford University Press, 1990).

4. Acid rain, hazardous chemicals, and chlorofluorocarbons are Worldwatch Institute estimates based on World Resources Institute, *World Resources 1990-91*; nuclear warheads from Swedish International Peace Research Institute, *SIPRI Yearbook 1990: World Armaments and Disarmament* (Oxford: Oxford University Press, 1990); radioactive waste is Worldwatch Institute estimate based on cumulative nuclear-power electricity production from International Atomic Energy Agency, *Nuclear Power Reactors in the World* (Vienna: 1991).

5. Brian Huntley et al., *South African Environments into the 21st Century* (Cape Town, South Africa: Human & Rousseau Tafelberg, 1989).

6. Parikh and Parikh, "Unsustainable Consumption Patterns."

7. Energy intensity and toxics emissions from Michael Renner, *Jobs in a Sustainable Economy*, Worldwatch Paper 104 (Washington, D.C.: Worldwatch Institute, September 1991); air pollution from U.S. Environmental Protection Agency, Office of Air Quality Planning and Standards, *National Air Pollution Estimates 1940-89* (Washington, D.C.: 1991).

8. Table 4-2 from United Nations, *1989 Energy Statistics Yearbook* (New York: 1991). Per capita consumption figures are easily misread to mean "personal consumption" when in fact they measure "societal consumption." Environmental damage per capita far exceeds environmental damage caused directly by an individual consumer's habits and choices. Household waste, for example, accounts for less than half the weight of all refuse in industrial countries. Per person greenhouse gas emissions exceed personal emissions from home and car by at least a factor of two. See James R. Udall, "Domestic Calculations," *Sierra*, July/August 1989, and more generally, Allan Schnaiberg, "The Political Economy of Consumption: Ecological Policy Limits," Northwestern University, Evanston, Ill., presented at American Association for the Advancement of Science Annual Meeting, Washington, D.C., February 1991.

9. Eric D. Larson, "Trends in the Consumption of Energy-Intensive Basic Materials in Industrialized Countries and Implications for Developing Regions," paper for International Symposium on Environmentally Sound Energy Technologies and Their Transfer to Developing Countries and European Economies in Transition, Milan, Italy, October 21-25, 1991; see also Eric D. Larson et al., "Beyond the Era of Materials," *Scientific American*, June 1986, and Robert H. Williams et al., "Materials, Affluence, and Industrial Energy Use," in Annual Reviews, Inc., *Annual Review of Energy 1987*, Vol. 12 (Palo Alto, Calif.: 1987).

10. Larson, "Trends in the Consumption of Energy-Intensive Basic Materials."

11. Worldwatch Institute estimates of world total consumption if all 5.5 billion people living in mid-1992 consumed on the levels of the consumer class assumes average consumer-class consumption of 3.5 tons of carbon emissions per capita per year as estimated from Marland et al., $CO_2$ *Emissions from Fossil Fuel Burning and Cement Manufacturing*, from Boden, private communication, from World Bank, *World Development Report 1991*, and from Sprout and Weaver, "1988 World Distribution of Income"; mining increase of 3.4 times estimated from annual iron and steel consumption of industrial countries of 470 kilograms per capita, compared with developing-country use of 36 kilograms per capita, from Parikh and Parikh, "Unsustainable Consumption Patterns"; logging increase estimated from industrial-country annual consumption of sawn wood per capita of 213 kilograms and developing-country use of 19 kilograms (3.3-fold), and from paper consumption of 148 kilograms and 11 kilograms respectively (3.5-fold), from ibid.

12. Auto from Robert B. Reich, *The Work of Nations: Preparing Ourselves for 21st Century Capitalism* (New York: Alfred A. Knopf, 1991).

13. Office of Promotion and Information for the Bataan Export Processing Zone, Philippines, "Remember Bataan?" advertisement in *Fortune*, October 1975.

14. Debt from Julia Michaels, "Brazil to Take New Tack on Debt," *Christian Science Monitor*, June 27, 1991; electricity use from Howard S. Geller, *Efficient Electricity Use: A Development Strategy for Brazil* (Washington, D.C.: American Council for an Energy-Efficient Economy, 1991).

15. El Salvador and Costa Rica is Worldwatch Institute estimate based on FAO, *Production Yearbook 1988* (Rome: 1989), and FAO, *Trade Yearbook 1988* (Rome: 1990); Japan's imports from Jim MacNeill et al., *Beyond Interdependence: The Meshing of the*

*World's Economy and the Earth's Ecology* (New York: Oxford University Press, 1991).

16. Netherlands National Committee for IUCN/Steering Group for World Conservation Strategy, *The Netherlands and the World Ecology*, cited in World Resources Institute, World Conservation Union, and United Nations Environment Programme, *Global Biodiversity Strategy* (Washington, D.C.: 1992).

17. MacNeill et al., *Beyond Interdependence*; grain from Alan Durning and Holly Brough, *Taking Stock: Animal Farming and the Environment*, Worldwatch Paper 103 (Washington, D.C.: Worldwatch Institute, July 1991).

18. Illegal wildlife from Debra Rose, "International Politics and Latin American Wildlife Resources," Department of Political Science, University of Florida, presented at the Sixteenth International Congress of the Latin American Studies Association, Washington, D.C., April 4-6, 1991; habitat destruction and species loss from John C. Ryan, "Conserving Biological Diversity," in Lester R. Brown et al., *State of the World 1992* (New York: W.W. Norton & Co., 1992); hunting and species extinction, and value of wildlife trade, from Sarah Fitzgerald, *International Wildlife Traffic: Whose Business Is It?* (Baltimore, Md.: World Wildlife Fund, 1989).

19. Butterflies, deer, and frogs from Fitzgerald, *International Wildlife Traffic*; frogs also from Radhakrishna Rao, "India: Bullfrog Extinction," *Third World Week* (Institute for Current World Affairs, Hanover, N.H.), November 23, 1990.

20. Area and wildlife affected from Stephanie Joyce, "Snorting Peru's Rain Forest," *International Wildlife*, May/June 1990, and from James Brooke, "Peruvian Farmers Razing Rain Forest to Sow Drug Crops," *New York Times*, August 13, 1989; steep slopes and chemical herbicides from Mark Mardon, "The Big Push," *Sierra*, November/December 1988.

21. Dourojeanni quoted in Brooke, "Peruvian Farmers Razing Rain Forest."

22. Herman Daly, "Environmental Impact Identity—Orders of Magnitude" (draft), World Bank, Washington, D.C., 1991; also see Ekins, "The Sustainable Consumer Society: A Contradiction in Terms?"

23. José Goldemberg et al., *Energy for a Sustainable World* (Washington, D.C.: World Resources Institute, 1987).

24. Ibid.; carbon dioxide reductions from Intergovernmental Panel on Climate Change, "Policymakers' Summary of the Scientific Assessment of Climate Change," Report to IPCC from Working Group I, Geneva, June 1990, and from U.S. Environmental

Protection Agency, *Policy Options for Stabilizing Global Climate* (draft) (Washington, D.C.: 1989).

## CHAPTER 5. Food and Drink

1. Hungry poor and undernourished poor estimated from World Bank, *World Development Report 1990* (New York: Oxford University Press, 1990), from Bread for the World, *Hunger 1992* (Washington, D.C.: 1991), and from Michael Lipton, *The Poor and the Poorest: Some Interim Findings*, Discussion Paper 25 (Washington, D.C.: World Bank, 1988); unsafe drinking water from United Nations Development Programme, *Human Development Report 1991* (New York: Oxford University Press, 1991); share of water-borne disease from G.A. Brown, "Keynote Address," in proceedings *World Water 1986* (London: Thomas Telford Ltd., 1987).

2. Alan Durning, *Poverty and the Environment: Reversing the Downward Spiral*, Worldwatch Paper 92 (Washington, D.C.: Worldwatch Institute, November 1989).

3. Middle-income diet and fat from Chen Junshi et al., *Diet, Lifestyle, and Mortality in China: A Study of the Characteristics of 65 Chinese Counties* (New York: Oxford University Press, 1990); a small share of middle-income class—the low-income residents of industrial countries—commonly have unhealthy, high-fat diets, see Alix M. Freedman, "Amid Ghetto Hunger, Many More Suffer Eating Wrong Foods," *Wall Street Journal*, December 18, 1990, "Fast-Food Chains Play Central Role in Diet of the Inner-City Poor," *Wall Street Journal*, December 19, 1990, and "An Inner-City Shopper Seeking Healthy Food Finds Offerings Scant," *Wall Street Journal*, December 20, 1990; beverage consumption from Frederick Clairmonte and John Cavanagh, *Merchants of Drink* (Penang, Malaysia: Third World Network, 1988).

4. Missing nutrients and storage from World Health Organization (WHO), *Diet, Nutrition and the Prevention of Chronic Diseases*, Technical Report Series 797 (Geneva: 1990), and from Junshi et al., *Diet, Life-style, and Mortality in China*; rice paddies and methane from Japan Environment Agency and U.S. Environmental Protection Agency, "Methane Emissions and Opportunities for Control: Workshop Results of Intergovernmental Panel on Climate Change, Response Strategies Working Group," Washington, D.C., September 1990.

5. Meat consumption is carcass weight, actual consumed weight is about two thirds as much; meat and fat consumption from Alan Durning and Holly Brough, *Taking Stock: Animal Farming and the Environment*, Worldwatch Paper 103 (Washington, D.C.: World-

watch Institute, July 1991). Table 5-1 from U.S. Department of
Agriculture (USDA), Foreign Agricultural Service (FAS),
"World Livestock Situation," Washington, D.C., April 1991,
and from Linda Bailey, agricultural economist, USDA, Washington, D.C., private communication, September 11, 1990. Authorities recommend 30-percent fat diet from National Research Council, *Diet and Health: Implications for Reducing Chronic Disease Risk* (Washington, D.C.: National Academy Press, 1989), from Gregory Byrne, "Surgeon General Takes Aim at Saturated Fats," *Science*, August 3, 1988, and from WHO, *Diet, Nutrition and the Prevention of Chronic Diseases.* Recent research includes Junshi et al., *Diet, Life-style, and Mortality in China*; see also Gail Vines, "China's Long March to Longevity," *New Scientist*, December 8, 1990), and Walter C. Willet et al., "Relation of Meat, Fat, and Fiber Intake to the Risk of Colon Cancer in a Prospective Study among Women," *New England Journal of Medicine*, December 13, 1990. Effects of excessive fat from Gina Kolata, "Report Urges Low-Fat Diet for Everyone," *New York Times*, February 28, 1990.

6. Grain to produce beef from Cattle-Fax, Inc., "Grain Utilization in the Livestock and Poultry Industries," Englewood, Colo., December 8, 1989; share of grain fed to livestock from USDA, FAS, "World Cereals Used for Feed" (unpublished printout), Washington, D.C., April 1991.

7. Environmental effects from Durning and Brough, *Taking Stock*; water use from Jim Oltjen, professor, Department of Animal Science, University of California, Davis, private communication, February 12, 1991; energy use from David Pimentel et al., "The Potential for Grass-Fed Livestock: Resource Constraints," *Science*, February 22, 1980, and from David Pimentel, professor, Cornell University, Ithaca, N.Y., private communication, February 22, 1991.

8. Durning and Brough, *Taking Stock*.

9. Share of farm subsidies for feed and livestock from Organisation for Economic Co-operation and Development (OECD), *Agricultural Policies, Markets and Trade: Monitoring and Outlook: 1991* (Paris: 1991); Public Voice for Food and Health Policy, Washington D.C., private communication, March 5, 1992; Earthsave, Felton, Calif., private communication, March 5, 1992; Johanna Wald and David Alberswerth, "Our Ailing Public Rangelands: Still Ailing! Condition Report 1989," National Wildlife Federation and Natural Resources Defense Council, Washington, D.C., and San Francisco, Calif., October 1989.

10. Food chain energy use from Pimentel, private communication,

except for share for animal agriculture, which is Worldwatch Institute estimate from Durning and Brough, *Taking Stock*.

11. Frozen-fresh comparison from David Pimentel, "Energy Flow in the Food System," in David Pimentel and Carl W. Hall, eds., *Food and Energy Resources* (Orlando, Fla.: Academic Press, 1984); U.S. potato consumption from "Potato Producers Finding Big Market in Frozen Fries," *Farmline*, October 1991; European frozen meals from Euromonitor Publications Ltd., *Consumer Europe 1986/87* (London: 1988) and *Consumer Europe 1991* (London: 1991); Japanese pizza from Euromonitor Publications Ltd., *Consumer Japan 1990* (London: 1990).

12. U.S. aluminum cans from John E. Young, "Aluminum's Real Tab," *World Watch*, March/April 1992; Japan's aluminum and cans from Merton J. Pecj, ed., *The World Aluminum Industry in a Changing Era* (Washington, D.C.: Resources for the Future, 1988); Japanese cartons from Hisao Kobata, "Domestic Consumption Boom Continues in Paper Industry," *Business Japan*, March 1991; U.S. food and beverage packaging as share of weight of municipal solid waste is Worldwatch Institute estimate based on U.S. Congress, Office of Technology Assessment (OTA), *Facing America's Trash: What's Next for Municipal Solid Waste* (Washington, D.C.: U.S. Government Printing Office, 1989), on Denis Dunham, "Food Cost Review, 1989," Economic Research Service, USDA, Washington, D.C., July 1990, and on EPA, Office of Solid Waste and Emergency Response, "Characterization of Municipal Solid Waste in the United States: 1990 Update," Washington, D.C., June 1990; food and beverage packaging as share by volume from OECD, *The State of the Environment, 1991* (Paris: 1991).

13. Robin Ashton, "Consumers Want it All," *Packaging*, June 1991.

14. Global beverage trends, global mean soft drink consumption, and share of drinks that are tap water from Clairmonte and Cavanagh, *Merchants of Drink*; U.S. 1990 soft drinks consumption from "The Battle for Your Business," *Consumer Reports*, August 1991; U.S. water consumption from *Beverage Industry*, Cleveland, Ohio, private communication, September 14, 1990.

15. Rising global soft drink consumption from United Nations Industrial Development Organization (UNIDO), *Industry and Development Global Report 1990/91* (Vienna: 1990); global spread of Coca-Cola and PepsiCo. from Clairmonte and Cavanagh, *Merchants of Drink*, from Guy de Jonquieres, "Home-grown Produce on the Multinationals' Shopping List" *Financial Times*, August 8, 1991, from "India's Wave of Fizz and Chips," *Asiaweek*, June 22, 1990, and from "Burma's New Fizz," *Asiaweek*,

October 4, 1991; non-U.S. share of Coca-Cola operating income and Keough quote from Roger Cohen, "For Coke, World is its Oyster," *New York Times*, November 21, 1991; "conquered the world" quote from *Adweek*, June 25, 1990.

16. Use of refillable bottles in developing countries from Scott Chaplin, "Packaging Trends Around the World: Implications for the United States" (draft), Rocky Mountain Institute, Old Snowmass, Colo., 1991.

17. Throwaway beverage containers is Worldwatch Institute estimate based on "Aluminum Recycling At All-Time High," *Journal of Commerce*, March 8, 1991, on John Elkington et al., *The Green Consumer* (New York: Viking Penguin, 1990), on Council for Solid Waste Solutions, Washington, D.C., private communication, June 14, 1991, and on UNIDO, *Industry and Development Global Report 1990/91*; Tetra-Pak from UNIDO, *Industry and Development Global Report*; share of throwaways in different regions from Chaplin, "Packaging Trends Around the World"; Japanese canned coffee and tea from "Pop-top Jive," *Asiaweek*, February 8, 1991.

18. "Wrapping Is a Rip Off!" from Women's Environmental Network, *Newsletter* (London), Spring 1991; author's observations in Esteli, Nicaragua, February-May 1986.

19. Refillable trends from Chaplin, "Packaging Trends Around the World."

20. Share of produce from California from Jeffrey Hollender, *How to Make the World a Better Place* (New York: William Morrow, 1990); transport/farm energy of lettuce from Pimentel, "Energy Flow in the Food System"; travel of average mouthful of food from U.S. Department of Defense, *U.S. Agriculture: Potential Vulnerabilities*, cited in Cornucopia Project, *Empty Breadbasket?* (Emmaus, Pa.: Rodale Press, 1981).

21. Soaring bottled-water consumption from UNIDO, *Industry and Development Global Report 1990-91*; impurity of bottled water from Ginia Bellafante, "Bottled Water; Fads and Facts," *Garbage Magazine*, January/February 1991; U.S. bottled water imports from Anthony Ramirez, "Now, From Brazil, 'Light' Water," *New York Times*, November 25, 1989; Steven Greenhouse, "Perrier's New American Assault," *New York Times*, October 30, 1988; United Nations General Assembly, Report of the Economic and Social Council, "Achievements of the International Drinking Water Supply and Sanitation Decade, 1981–1990," New York, July 13, 1990.

22. Kilometers driven for shopping from OTA, *Technology and the American Economic Transition*; supermarket number and size and

convenience stores from Paul Kaufman and Doris J. Newton, "Trends in Grocery Retailing Concentration," *National Food Review* (USDA), October/December 1990; goods in stock from Patricia Sellers, "Winning Over the New Consumer," *Fortune*, July 29, 1991.

23. John Davies, "Cherries Queue for Japan," *Journal of Commerce*, June 18, 1991; Chile grapes from Lovell S. Jarvis, Department of Agricultural Economics, University of California, Davis, "Chilean Fruit Development Since 1973: Manipulating the Cornucopia to What End?" paper prepared for the Sixteenth International Congress of the Latin American Studies Association, Washington, D.C., April 4-6, 1991, and from Bradley Graham, "South American Grapes: Tale of Two Countries," *Washington Post*, February 2, 1988; Brazilian orange juice from U.N. Economic Commission for Latin America and the Caribbean (ECLAC), *Changing Production Patterns with Social Equity* (Santiago, Chile: 1991); European fruit from Jarvis, "Chilean Fruit Development Since 1973"; flowers from Sarita Kendall, "Colombian Flower Power Blooms," *Financial Times*, September 19, 1991.

24. Malaysian cocoa from Martha McDevitt, "Cocoa—Not a Sweet Story," *Bethesda Coop News* (Bethesda, Md.), February 1991; beef from Durning and Brough, *Taking Stock*.

25. Don Hinrichsen, *Our Common Seas* (London: Earthscan, 1990).

26. Shrimp production and mangroves from ibid.; Ecuador's shrimp exports to U.S. and Japan from ECLAC, *Changing Production Patterns with Social Equity*; Philippines from Robin Broad and John Cavanagh, "Marcos' Ghost," *Amicus Journal*, Fall 1989; blue fin and red fish from Ken Hinman, executive director, National Coalition for Marine Conservation, Savannah, Ga., private communication, February 11, 1992.

27. Massachusetts Department of Food and Agriculture, *The Massachusetts Farm-and-Food System: A Five-Year Policy Framework, 1989-93* (Boston: 1988); New York from "Food for Thought," *Metropolis*, July/August 1991.

28. Advantages of farm markets from Hollender, *How to Make the World A Better Place*; college food buying from Holly Brough, "Environmental Studies: Is It Academic?" *World Watch*, January/February 1992.

29. Paul Ekins, "Growing Concern," (Manchester) *Guardian*, January 13, 1988.

30. Harriet Parcells, "Big Trucks Getting a Free Ride," National Association of Railroad Passengers, Washington D.C., April 1990.

31. Energy required to feed whole world in consumer-class style estimated by Worldwatch Institute using U.S. energy use for food and drinks as typical for consumer class, based on Pimentel, private communication, and on United Nations, *1989 Energy Statistics Yearbook* (New York: 1991). For a basic-needs energy scenario including hot water, refrigeration, and modern cooking devices, see José Goldemberg et al., *Energy for Development* (Washington, D.C.: World Resources Institute, 1987).

## CHAPTER 6. Clean Motion

1. History of speed and Valéry quote from Ivan Illich, *Toward a History of Needs* (Berkeley, Calif.: Heyday Books, 1977); speed of jets from Don Hanson, media relations, McDonell Douglas, Long Beach, Calif., private communication, February 21, 1992; see also John Maxwell Hamilton, *Entangling Alliances: How the Third World Shapes Our Lives* (Cabin John, Md.: Seven Locks Press, 1990).
2. Energy intensities of ground transport from Marcia D. Lowe, *Alternatives to the Automobile: Transport for Livable Cities*, Worldwatch Paper 98 (Washington, D.C.: Worldwatch Institute, October 1990); air travel from U.S. Department of Energy (DOE), Energy Information Administration (EIA), *Annual Energy Review 1990* (Washington, D.C.: 1991).
3. Author's observation, Pilcomaya, Bolivia, May 1988.
4. Marcia D. Lowe, *The Bicycle: Vehicle for A Small Planet*, Worldwatch Paper 90 (Washington, D.C.: Worldwatch Institute, September 1989).
5. Table 6-1, for 1988 or most recent prior year, calculated from International Roads Federation, *World Roads Statistics 1984-88* (Geneva: 1989), and from Population Reference Bureau, *World Population Data Sheet* (Washington, D.C.: various years).
6. International car ownership from Euromonitor Publications, Ltd., *International Marketing Data and Statistics 1986/87* (London: 1988); overall, 60 percent of households in western industrial countries have cars, according to Organisaton for Economic Co-operation and Development (OECD), *State of the Environment, 1991* (Paris: 1991); Japanese 1970 car ownership from Sepp Linhart, "From Industrial to Postindustrial Society: Changes in Japanese Leisure-Related Values and Behavior," *Journal of Japanese Studies*, Summer 1988; Japanese 1988 car ownership from Euromonitor Publications Ltd., *Consumer Japan 1990* (London: 1990); French two-car households from OECD, *State of the Environment, 1991*; U.S. two-car households from

Motor Vehicle Manufacturers Association (MVMA), *Facts and Figures '91* (Detroit, Mich.: 1991); two-car garages from "Motor Motels," *American Demographics,* April 1989.

7. Quoted in Paul Wachtel, *The Poverty of Affluence* (Philadelphia: New Society Publishers, 1989).

8. Range Rovers from T.R. Reid, "U.S. Automakers Grind Gears in Japan," *Washington Post,* September 23, 1990; Jeeps from "On the Road," *India Today,* August 15, 1991; car acceleration, truck sales, and fuel economy from Warren Brown, "Study: Car Buyers Stall Effort to Save Fuel," *Washington Post,* October 18, 1991; trucks' share of vehicles from MVMA, *Facts and Figures '91*; large cars in Europe from OECD, *State of the Environment, 1991*; BMW in Japan from *Japan Economic Journal,* September 8, 1990.

9. World auto fleet in 1992 is Worldwatch Institute estimate based on MVMA, *Facts and Figures '91*, and on 1991 production estimate from Kevin Done, "Prepare for Rising Demand in Less Developed Countries," *Financial Times* (London), September 11, 1991; traffic fatalities, carbon emissions, air pollution, and acid rain from Lowe, *Alternatives to the Automobile*.

10. Automobile consumption of world petroleum is Worldwatch Institute estimate based on share of crude oil converted to motor gasoline worldwide, excluding diesel fuel consumed by passenger cars, based on United Nations, *1989 Energy Statistics Yearbook* (New York: 1991); auto manufacturing energy from Mary Holcomb et al., eds., *Transportation Energy Data Book: Edition 9* (Oak Ridge, Tenn.: Oak Ridge National Laboratories, 1987); energy and toxics ranks from Michael Renner, *Jobs in a Sustainable Economy,* Worldwatch Paper 104 (Washington, D.C.: Worldwatch Institute, September 1991).

11. Materials in car from MVMA, *Facts and Figures '91*; energy and toxics rank from Renner, *Jobs in A Sustainable Economy,* using "primary metals manufacturing" for metals, and "chemicals" for plastics.

12. Urban area for automobile in U.S. cities from Kirkpatrick Sale, *Human Scale* (New York: Coward, McCann, & Geoghegan, 1980); U.S. paved area—16 million hectares—from Michael Renner, *Rethinking the Role of the Automobile,* Worldwatch Paper 84 (Washington, D.C.: Worldwatch Institute, June 1988); road networks expansion from OECD, *State of the Environment, 1991*.

13. San Francisco commuting from U.S. Congress, Office of Technology Assessment (OTA), *Technology and the American Economic Transition* (Washington, D.C.: U.S. Government Printing Office, 1988); U.S. and Soviet commuting time from John S.

Robinson, "How Americans Use Time," *The Futurist*, September/October 1991.

14. Linhart, "From Industrial to Postindustrial Society."

15. Driving hours from John P. Robinson, "Americans on the Road," *American Demographics*, September 1989; air conditioning in 1990 from MVMA, *Facts and Figures '91*; air conditioning in 1960 from Robert J. Samuelson, "The Chilling of America," *Washington Post*, June 6, 1991; impact of chlorofluorocarbons on climate change from Center for Transportation Research, Argonne National Laboratory, *Emissions of Greenhouse Gases from the Use of Transportation Fuels and Electricity*, Vol. 2, Technical Appendices (Washington, D.C.: U.S. Department of Energy, 1991); compact disk players from Matthew Wald, "How Dreams of Clean Air Get Stuck in Traffic," *New York Times*, March 11, 1990; microwaves from "Harper's Index," *Harper's*, May 1991; telephones, of which there are already 5 million in U.S. cars, from Yuji Morikawa, "Portable Telephones Enter Phase of Fierce Competition," *Business Japan*, March 1991; carcooning from Marcia Lowe, senior researcher, Worldwatch Institute, Washington, D.C., private communication, February 6, 1992.

16. Passenger numbers and ticket sales from Mark Barrett, "Aircraft Pollution: Environmental Impacts and Future Solutions," World Wide Fund for Nature, Gland, Switzerland, August 1991; 1950 passenger kilometers from United Nations (UN), *Statistical Yearbook, 1953* (New York: 1954); 1990 passenger kilometers from UN, *Statistical Yearbook, 1987* (New York: 1990), with updates from UN, *Monthly Bulletin of Statistics*, various issues; U.S domestic travel from Air Transport Association, Washington, D.C., private communication, September 12, 1990.

17. Energy intensities of travel from DOE, EIA, *Annual Energy Review 1990;* shifting shares of transport modes from OTA, *Technology and the American Economic Transition*.

18. Carbon dioxide from Barrett, "Aircraft Pollution: Environmental Impacts and Future Solutions"; effects of nitrogen from ibid. and from Robert A. Egli, "Nitrogen Oxide Emissions from Air Traffic," *Chimia*, November 1990.

19. Stockholm from author's observations, May 1991; Portland and Toronto from Marcia D. Lowe, *Shaping Cities: The Human and Environmental Dimensions*, Worldwatch Paper 105 (Washington, D.C.: Worldwatch Institute, October 1991).

20. Mark Skinner, Boston, Mass., private communication, December 31, 1991; Michael Replogle from Jeff Mullen, Program As-

sistant, Institute for Transportation and Development Policy, Washington, D.C., private communication, February 10, 1992.

21. Company cars from "Queering the Motor Market," *Economist,* January 5, 1991; Friends of the Earth, "Traffic Free Towns! A Strategy for Local Groups Campaigning," London, August 1991; Alperson from Al-Ameen Kafaar, "Bicycle Brigade Seeks Better Deal for Pedal Power," *Star* (Johannesburg), September 14, 1991; Dutko from Joe Garner, "Activist Peddling Bike Rights," *Rocky Mountain News*, September 3, 1991; Swedish air travel tax from Jan Lothigius, "Cleaner Aero Engines Taking Off," *Enviro*, November 1991.

22. Tooker Gomberg of Edmonton from Bicycle Federation of America, "Street Theater Drama Aimed at Auto Users," *Bike News*, October 1990; Ricardo Neves, Institute of Technology for the Citizen, Rio de Janeiro, Brazil, private communication, February 12, 1990; Hamburg from Reinhold Pape, "Taking to the Streets," *Acid News*, December 1991.

## CHAPTER 7. The Stuff of Life

1. Wendell Berry, *Home Economics* (San Francisco: North Point Press, 1987).

2. Energy use of materials sector, a conservative estimate, is by Worldwatch Institute for 1988 and counts both mining and manufacturing energy, but excludes aspects such as timber extraction, minerals transportation, and petroleum products used as chemical feedstocks, based on Department of Energy (DOE), Energy Information Administration (EIA), *Manufacturing Energy Consumption Survey: Consumption of Energy 1988* (Washington, D.C.: U.S. Government Printing Office, 1991), and on U.S. Department of Commerce, Bureau of the Census, *1987 Census of Minerals Industries* (Washington, D.C.: U.S. Government Printing Office, 1990); total U.S. energy use in 1988 from DOE, EIA, *Annual Energy Review 1989* (Washington, D.C.: 1990); toxic emissions as share of all manufacturing toxic emissions are as reported to the U.S. Toxic Release Inventory of the Environmental Protection Agency, cited in Michael Renner, *Jobs in a Sustainable Economy*, Worldwatch Paper 104 (Washington, D.C.: Worldwatch Institute, September 1991).

3. Alan Durning, *Poverty and the Environment: Reversing the Downward Spiral*, Worldwatch Paper 92 (Washington, D.C.: Worldwatch Institute, November 1989).

4. Table 7-1 from U.S. Department of Commerce, Bureau of the Census, *Statistical Abstract of the United States: 1990* (Washington,

D.C.: U.S. Government Printing Office, 1990); U.N. Food and Agriculture Organization, *1961-1989 Wood and Wood Products* (Rome: 1991); 1990 cement production—fairly close to consumption because cement is traded little compared with other minerals—from Gail Mason, U.S. Department of the Interior, Bureau of Mines, Washington, D.C., private communication, January 13, 1992; Population Reference Bureau, *World Population Data Sheet* (Washington, D.C.: various years).

5. Steel is produced from iron, manganese, chromium, nickel, and molybdenum, estimated from John E. Young, "Mining the Earth," in Lester R. Brown et al., *State of the World 1992* (New York: W.W. Norton & Co., 1992). Cement's energy intensity exceeds even petroleum refining. Cement's share of carbon emissions count only industrial sources—fossil fuels and cement production; biological sources are excluded because of scientific uncertainties. Paper mills from Renner, *Jobs in a Sustainable Economy*.

6. Materials consumption thresholds estimated from sources used to compile Table 7-1.

7. Ivan Illich, *Toward a History of Needs* (Berkeley, Calif.: Heyday Books, 1977); U.S. per capita consumption of materials is Worldwatch Institute estimate based on petroleum and coal from DOE, EIA, *Annual Energy Review 1988* (Washington, D.C.: 1989), on other minerals and agricultural products from Bureau of the Census, *Statistical Abstract of the United States: 1990*, and on forest products from Alice Ulrich, *U.S. Timber Production, Trade, Consumption, and Price Statistics 1950-87* (Washington, D.C.: Forest Service, U.S. Department of Agriculture, 1989).

8. Mining and rivers from Young, "Mining the Earth"; chemicals output from Robert Ayres, "Eco-Restructuring: Managing the Transition to an Ecologically Sustainable Economy," Carnegie Mellon University, Pittsburgh, Penn., presented at American Association for the Advancement of Science Annual Meeting, Washington, D.C., February 18, 1991.

9. Lily Tomlin, *Lily Tomlin on Stage*, Arista Records, Inc., New York, 1977.

10. Expenditures for packaging from U.S. Congress, Office of Technology Assessment (OTA), *Facing America's Trash: What Next for Municipal Solid Waste?* (Washington, D.C.: U.S. Government Printing Office, 1989); U.K. packaging energy from Peter Bunyard and Fern Morgan-Greenville, eds., *The Green Alternative Guide to Good Living* (London: Methuen London Ltd., 1987); German packaging share of paper production for

1986 from Renate Kroesa, *Greenpeace Guide to Paper* (Washington, D.C.: Greenpeace, 1990); packaging share of plastics from Anita Glazer Sadun et al., "Breaking Down the Degradable Plastics Scam," Center for the Biology of Natural Systems, Queens College, City University of New York, report prepared for Greenpeace, 1990; packaging share, by volume, of solid waste from Organisation for Economic Co-operation and Development (OECD), *State of the Environment, 1991* (Paris: 1991); Chinese industry from Zhai Feng, "Better Packaging Boosts Business," *China Daily*, June 24, 1991.

11. Diapers from Karen Christensen, independent researcher, Boulder, Colo., private communication, October 18, 1990; Steve Usdin, "Snap Happy: Throwaway Cameras Are an Instant Hit," *Intersect*, June 1990; promotional batteries from "Batteries Electrify Company Promotional Campaigns," *Japanese Economic Journal*, September 8, 1990; razors from Cheryl Russell, "Guilty as Charged," *American Demographics*, February 1989; U.S. batteries from John Holusha, "Keeping a Gadget-Mad Nation Charged Up—and Safe," *New York Times*, September 22, 1991; styrofoam "peanuts" from EarthWorks Group, *50 Simple Things Your Business Can Do to Save the Earth* (Berkeley, Calif.: 1991); spray paint from Harold T. Pehr, president, Shellwick Industries, Leawood, Kans., letter to Worldwatch Institute (undated, 1991); paper and plastic ware are Worldwatch Institute estimates based on Environmental Protection Agency, Office of Solid Waste and Emergency Response, "Characterization of Municipal Solid Waste in the United States: 1990 Update," Washington, D.C., June 1990; throwaway video cassette of the Philmax company of Owings Mills, Md., from "News and New Products," *The Green Consumer Letter* (Tilden Press, Washington, D.C.), June 1990.

12. Tim Hunkin, "Things People Throw Away," *New Scientist*, December 31, 1988.

13. OECD, *Product Durability and Product Life Extension: Their Contribution to Solid Waste Management* (Paris: 1982).

14. Japanese appliances from Yorimoto Katsumi, "Tokyo's Serious Waste Problem," *Japan Quarterly*, July/September 1990; German appliances from Andrew Fisher, "Reincarnation in the Design Studio," *Financial Times*, April 3, 1991; televisions from Rhode Island Waste Management Corporation, "Annual Report 1986," cited in Jeffrey Hollender, *How to Make the World A Better Place* (New York: William Morrow, 1990); tires from U.S. Senate, Subcommittee on Energy Regulation and Conservation, in "Vital Signs," *World Watch*, September/October 1991.

15. Oscar Wilde, "Suitable Dress for Women Workers"; fashion's pace from OTA, *Technology and the American Economic Transition* (Washington, D.C.: U.S. Government Printing Office, 1988); Louis Cheskin of the Color Research Institute quoted in Vance Packard, *The Waste Makers* (New York: Pocket Books, Inc., 1964).

16. Spencer S. Hsu, "The Sneaker Steps Out," *Washington Post*, July 22, 1990.

17. Cotton farmers and pesticides from World Health Organization and United Nations Environment Programme, "Public Health Impact of Pesticide Use in Agriculture," Geneva and Nairobi, 1989; cotton and water from U.S. Department of Commerce, Bureau of the Census, *1987 Census of Agriculture, Vol. 3, Part 1, Farm and Ranch Irrigation Survey 1988* (Washington, D.C.: U.S. Government Printing Office, 1990); dyes and hazardous materials from Charles Austin, industrial hygienist, Amalgamated Clothing and Textile Workers Union, New York, private communication, February 24, 1992.

18. Esprit pamphlet, San Francisco, Calif., Fall 1990.

19. Julia Preston, "Gold Rush Brings Mercury Poisoning to Amazon," *Washington Post*, February 17, 1992; Alan Durning, *Apartheid's Environmental Toll*, Worldwatch Paper 95 (Washington, D.C.: Worldwatch Institute, May 1990); Action Alert, "The Destruction of the Okavango, Botswana," Econet (computer network), January 7, 1991.

20. Laura Ingalls Wilder, *Little House on the Prairie* (New York: Harper Trophy Books, 1941).

21. General Mining Act and reform attempts from "Cracks in Hard Rock," *Clementine* (Minerals Policy Center, Washington, D.C.), Spring 1991.

22. Association of Forest Service Employees for Environmental Ethics, Eugene, Oreg., private communication, February 21, 1992; Canada from Mark Cheater, "Save that Taiga," *World Watch*, July/August 1991.

23. Quoted in Alice Rawsthorn, "No Frills, No Spills," *Financial Times*, July 31, 1991.

24. German waste reduction and packaging reforms from Turner T. Smith and Lucas Bergkamp, "Packaging Waste Developments in Europe," *International Environment Reporter*, September 25, 1991; David Gardner et al., "Green Germany Drags Brussels," *Financial Times*, January 24, 1992.

25. Incinerators waste of energy from John Young, "Burn Out," *World Watch*, July/August 1991; Connets from *Waste Not* (Work on Waste USA, Inc., Canton, N.Y.), various issues; Washington

state from John E. Young, *Discarding the Throwaway Society*, Worldwatch Paper 101 (Washington, D.C.: Worldwatch Institute, January 1991); Seattle 1991 recycling rate from Jenny Bagby, economist, Seattle Solid Waste Utility, Seattle, Wash., private communication, February 10, 1992.

26. Glyn Roberts, "Tools for Self Reliance," *Resurgence*, November/ December 1991.

27. Everything Goes Furniture from "A Cluster of Eco-Villages," *In Context*, Summer 1991; Urban Ore from Information Services Department, Urban Ore, Inc., Berkeley, Calif., private communication, February 27, 1992; National Association of Dumpster Divers and Urban Miners, *The NADDUM News* (Big Fork, Mont.), various editions.

## CHAPTER 8. The Myth of Consume or Decline

1. Pleas to spend from Henry Allen, "Bye-Bye America's Pie," *Washington Post*, February 11, 1992; Range Rover quoted in Nick Ravo, "For the 90's, Lavish Amounts of Stinginess," *New York Times*, January 15, 1992.

2. Consumer expenditures and gross national product from Eva Pomice and Dana Hawkins, "The New Fear of Buying," *U.S. News & World Report*, March 4, 1991; see also Allan Schnaiberg, "The Political Economy of Consumption: Ecological Policy Limits," Northwestern University, Evanston, Ill., presented at American Association for the Advancement of Science Annual Meeting, Washington, D.C., February 1991.

3. First World consumption and developing countries from, for example, Lawrence Summers, "Research Challenges for Development Economists," *Finance and Development*, September 1991; least developed countries from United Nations Conference on Trade and Development, *The Least Developed Countries 1991 Report* (New York: United Nations, 1992); see also John Maxwell Hamilton, *Entangling Alliances: How the Third World Shapes Our Lives* (Cabin John, Md.: Seven Locks Press, 1990).

4. Michael Renner, *Jobs in a Sustainable Economy*, Worldwatch Paper 104 (Washington, D.C.: Worldwatch Institute, September 1991).

5. Auto subsidies from Marcia D. Lowe, *Reshaping Cities: The Human and Environmental Dimensions*, Worldwatch Paper 105 (Washington, D.C.: Worldwatch Institute, October 1991); energy subsidies from Mark Kosmo, *Money to Burn? The High Costs of Energy Subsidies* (Washington, D.C.: World Resources Institute, 1987); mining subsidies from John E. Young, "Mining the

Earth," in Lester R. Brown et al., *State of the World 1992* (New York: W.W. Norton & Co., 1992); timber subsidies from Robert Repetto, *The Forest for the Trees? Government Policies and the Misuse of Forest Resources* (Washington, D.C.: World Resources Institute, 1988); grain-fed livestock subsidies from Alan Durning and Holly Brough, *Taking Stock: Animal Farming and the Environment*, Worldwatch Paper 103 (Washington, D.C.: Worldwatch Institute, July 1991); minerals on U.S. federal land from John Young, "Free-Loding Off Uncle Sam," *World Watch*, January/February 1992; logging roads from Richard E. Rice, *The Uncounted Costs of Logging* (Washington, D.C.: The Wilderness Society, 1989); irrigation water from E. Phillip LeVeen and Laura B. King, *Turning Off the Tap on Federal Water Subsidies, Vol. 1* (San Francisco: Natural Resources Defense Council and California Rural Legal Assistance Foundation, 1985); French nuclear from François Nectoux, "Crisis in the French Nuclear Industry," Greenpeace International, Amsterdam, February 1991; Russian oil from Sylvia Nasar, "Can Capitalism Save the Ozone?" *New York Times*, February 7, 1992; U.K. cars from Malcolm Fergusson, "Subsidized Pollution: Company Cars and the Greenhouse Effect," report prepared for Greenpeace UK, London, January 1990; Quebec aluminum from John Young, "Aluminum's Real Tab," *World Watch*, March/April 1992; Japan feed-grain from Bengt Hyberg et al., *The World Coarse Grain Market—Government Intervention and Multilateral Policy Reform* (Washington, D.C.: U.S. Department of Agriculture, 1990).

6. Environmental taxes from Sandra Postel and Christopher Flavin, "Reshaping the Global Economy," in Lester R. Brown et al., *State of the World 1991* (New York: W.W. Norton & Co., 1991).

7. Ibid.; Renner, *Jobs in a Sustainable Economy*.

8. European Community carbon tax from David Lascelles, "A Mission to Make the Polluters Pay," *Financial Times*, January 28, 1992.

9. Poverty alleviation strategies from Alan Durning, *Poverty and the Environment: Reversing the Downward Spiral*, Worldwatch Paper 92 (Washington, D.C.: Worldwatch Institute, November 1989), from World Bank, *World Development Report 1990* (New York: Oxford University Press, 1990), and from United Nations Development Programme, *Human Development Report 1991* (New York: Oxford University Press, 1991).

10. Robert Goodland and Herman Daly, "Ten Reasons Why Northern Income Growth Is Not the Solution to Southern Pov-

erty" (draft), Environment Department, World Bank, Washington, D.C., February 1992.

11. Stumpf quoted in Allen, "Bye-Bye America's Pie."
12. Juliet Schor, *The Overworked American: The Unexpected Decline of Leisure* (New York: Basic Books, 1992).
13. Renner, *Jobs in a Sustainable Economy*; increase in work since 1970 from Schor, *The Overworked American.*
14. Schor, *The Overworked American.*
15. Ibid.
16. European and Japanese work hours from Renner, *Jobs in a Sustainable Economy*; TV viewing from George Comstock, *Television in America* (Beverly Hills, Calif.: Sage Publications, 1980), and from Sepp Linhart, "From Industrial to Postindustrial Society: Changes in Japanese Leisure-Related Values and Behavior," *Journal of Japanese Studies*, Summer 1988; Leach quoted in Schor, *The Overworked American.*
17. Shor, *The Overworked American.*
18. Family leave campaign from Women's Legal Defense Fund, Washington, D.C., private communication, March 2, 1992; voluntary worktime reduction programs from Barney Olmsted, codirector, New Ways to Work, San Francisco, Calif., private communication, March 3, 1992.
19. Olmsted, private communication; *karoshi* from Louise do Rosario, "Dropping in Harness," *Far Eastern Economic Review*, April 25, 1991; young Japanese and European union demands from Schor, *The Overworked American*; Japan's five-day week plan from Linhart, "From Industrial to Postindustrial Society."
20. Shor, *The Overworked American.*

## CHAPTER 9. The Cultivation of Needs

1. Ivan Illich, *Toward a History of Needs* (Berkeley, Calif.: Heyday Books, 1977).
2. Mark Landler et al., "What Happened to Advertising?" *Business Week*, September 23, 1991; chair lifts from Paula Span, "Ads: They're Everywhere!" *Washington Post*, April 28, 1990; classrooms and doctors offices from Randall Rothenberg, "Two Views on Whittle's TV Reports," *New York Times*, June 1, 1990; feature films from Randall Rothenberg, "Messages From Sponsors Become Harder to Detect," *New York Times*, November 19, 1989; merit badges from "Harper's Index," *Harper's*, April 1991.
3. Paula J. Silbey, "Merchants Star on Mall's Video Wall," *Shopping Centers Today*, August 1989; closed-circuit television at bus stops and subway stations from Span, "Ads: They're Everywhere!";

closed-circuit television at exercise clubs and ski resorts from Janice Kelly, "Out-of-home Builds," *Advertising Age*, September 16, 1991; television at checkout lines from "Turner Aims to Line Up Captive Audience," *Wall Street Journal*, June 21, 1991; hot dogs from Span, "Ads: They're Everywhere!"; "Which Came First? Adman or Egg?" *Fortune*, April 9, 1990; Coca-Cola from William J. Broad, "Almost Broke, Soviet Union's Space Efforts Go on Sale," *New York Times*, September 3, 1991.

4. Kim quoted in Annetta Miller, "You Are What You Buy," *Newsweek*, June 4, 1990.

5. People able to remember few ads from James D. Norris, *Advertising and the Transformation of American Society, 1865–1920* (Westport, Conn.: Greenwood Publishing Co., 1990); cumulative effect from Ronald Berman, *Advertising and Social Change* (Beverly Hills, Calif.: Sage Publications, 1985).

6. Advertising executive quoted in Paul Wachtel, *The Poverty of Affluence* (Philadelphia: New Society Publishers, 1989); Puckett quoted in Vance Packard, *The Waste Makers* (New York: Pocket Books, Inc., 1964).

7. Monetary figures are adjusted for inflation and expressed in 1989 dollars; U.S. 1950 per capita from U.S. Department of Commerce, *Historical Statistics of the United States, Colonial Times to 1970, Bicentennial Edition, Part 2* (Washington, D.C.: 1975), and from U.S. Department of Commerce, Bureau of the Census, *Statistical Abstract of the United States: 1990* (Washington, D.C.: U.S. Government Printing Office, 1990); U.S. 1990 per capita from Crain Communications, Inc., Chicago, Ill., private communication, January 17, 1992, and from Census Bureau, Suitland, Md., private communication, January 13, 1992; world per capita from Robert J. Coen, *International Herald Tribune*, October 10, 1984, cited in Frederick Clairmonte and John Cavanagh, *Merchants of Drink* (Penang, Malaysia: Third World Network, 1988), and from Tracy Poltie, International Advertising Association, New York, private communication, January 15, 1992; advertising growth faster than economic output based on Angus Maddison, *The World Economy in the 20th Century* (Paris: Organisation for Economic Co-operation and Development, 1989); Figure 9-1 from Poltie, private communication, August 29, 1990, with population figures from U.S. Department of Commerce, Bureau of the Census, *Statistical Abstract of the United States* (Washington, D.C.: U.S. Government Printing Office, various years), and from Population Reference Bureau, *1988 World Population Data Sheet* (Washington, D.C.: 1988); Prakash Chandra, "India: Middle-Class Spending," *Third World Week* (Institute for Current World Affairs, Hanover, N.H.), March 2, 1990; Korea from "Asia's

Network Boom," *Asiaweek*, July 6, 1990; quote from Guy de Jonquieres, "Home-grown Produce on the Multinationals' Shopping List," *Financial Times*, August 8, 1991.

8. Child marketer quote from Herbert I. Schiller, *Culture, Inc.* (New York: Oxford University Press, 1989); Japan information and Hideo and Keng quotes from "Hey, Little Spender," *Asiaweek*, December 6, 1991.

9. Children's market is defined as expenditures by or for those aged 4–12, from Peter Newcomb, "Hey, Dude, Let's Consume," *Forbes*, June 11, 1990; ad spending on children and cartoon-centered toys from Deborah Baldwin, "Read This," *Common Cause Magazine*, May/June 1991; clubs from Christopher Power, "Getting 'Em While They're Young," *Business Week*, September 9, 1991; Mattel quote and Barbie accessories from Karen Zagor, "Barbie Picks Her Accessories," *Financial Times*, February 21, 1991; Barbie departments from Kate Fitzgerald, "Mattel Fashions Barbie Boutique," *Advertising Age*, July 1, 1991.

10. Ads account for about one third of U.S. mail from Richard Leiby, "The Junk Mail Plague: You Can Run, But You Can't Hide," *Washington Post*, April 22, 1991; 13.6 billion catalogs from EarthWorks Group, *50 Simple Things Your Business Can Do to Save the Earth* (Berkeley, Calif.: 1991); newspaper advertising from Andrew Sullivan, "Buying and Nothingness," book review in *The New Republic*, May 8, 1989; Canadian forests felled for U.S. newspaper advertisements is Worldwatch Institute estimate, based on volume of Canada's timber harvest used for pulpwood from Jacques Lepage, *Statistics Canada* (Ottawa: Ministry of Supply and Services Canada, 1990), on harvested area from Forestry Canada, *The State of Forestry in Canada, 1990 Report to Parliament* (Ottawa: Ministry of Supply and Services Canada, 1991), on volume of newsprint exported from Canada to the United States and share of U.S. newsprint consumption for newspapers from American Paper Institute, Newsprint Division, "Monthly Statistics Report," New York, December 1991, and on share of advertising in U.S. newspapers from Sullivan, "Buying and Nothingness"; McCrory quote from Mark Cheater, "Save that Taiga," *World Watch*, July/August 1991.

11. David Briars, Craftsbury, Vt., private communication, Fall 1991.

12. Tobacco ads are or soon will be banned throughout the West from "European Tobacco Ads," *Wall Street Journal*, May 21, 1990, and from "Single Marketing," *Economist*, March 24, 1990.

13. Howard Kurtz, "Bush May Let Children's TV Measure

Become Law," *Washington Post*, October 3, 1990; Action for Children's Television, Boston, Mass., private communication, October 17, 1990; European Community from Jeannine Johnson, "In Search of . . . the European T.V. Show," *Europe*, November 1989, and from Gary Mead, "Not in Front of the Children," *Financial Times*, December 19, 1991.

14. Australia from *IOCU Newsletter* (International Organization of Consumer Unions, Malaysia), No. 8, 1990; "Ban TV Food Ads Targeting Young," *Washington Post*, July 24, 1991.

15. "Free Tree. Plant it for the Planet." advertisement, *Washington Post*, April 18, 1991; tree/gasoline carbon comparison is Worldwatch Institute estimate based on life-cycle carbon emissions per gallon of gasoline, from Gregg Marland, "Carbon Dioxide Emission Rates for Conventional and Synthetic Fuels," *Energy*, Vol. 8, No. 12, 1983, and on average tree seedling carbon fixation, from Astrid Guttman, "Urban Releaf," *World Watch*, November/December 1989.

16. U.S. situation from Jaclyn Fierman, "The Big Muddle in Green Marketing," *Fortune*, June 3, 1991; "Environmental Advertising Code," *Environmental News from the Netherlands*, Ministry of Housing, Physical Planning and Environment, The Hague, Netherlands, 1991; "Labelling—New Environmental Consumerism Program Approved by French Council of Ministers," *International Environment Reporter*, July 3, 1991; action by 10 states from Joanne S. Lublin, "Environment Claims Are Sowing More Confusion, 2 Reports Say," *Wall Street Journal*, November 8, 1990; Europe and North America from Peter Weber, "Green Seals of Approval Heading to Market," *World Watch*, July/August 1990; Japan from Denis Hayes, "Harnessing Market Forces to Protect the Earth," *Issues in Science and Technology*, Winter 1990–91.

17. McDonald's and Procter & Gamble from Stephan Schmidheiny, *Changing Course: A Global Business Perspective on Development and the Environment* (Cambridge, Mass.: The MIT Press, 1992).

18. Randall Bloomquist, "Commercial Break," *Utne Reader*, January/February 1992.

19. Time spent watching television in U.S. and Japan from George Comstock, *Television in America* (Beverly Hills, Calif.: Sage Publications, 1985), and from John P. Robinson, "I Love My TV," *American Demographics*, September 1990; time in U.K. from Paul Ekins, "The Sustainable Consumer Society: A Contradiction in Terms?" *International Environmental Affairs*, Fall 1991.

20. Reilly quoted in *Fortune*, March 26, 1990; increased commercialization of broadcasting from Sydney W. Head, *World Broadcasting Systems: A Comparative Analysis* (Belmont, Calif.: Wadsworth, 1985); International Advertising Association quoted in Schiller, *Culture, Inc.*

21. Breakup of monopolies from Edward S. Herman, "The Deepening Market in the West: (3) Commercial Broadcasting on the March," *Zeta*, May 1990, from Raymond Snoddy, "The Changing Face of European T.V.," *Europe*, April 1988, and from Sullivan, "Buying and Nothingness"; European Community (EC) unified broadcast region from Johnson, "In Search of . . . the European T.V. Show"; Europe TV market a bonanza from Kevin Cote, "European Advertisers Prepare for 1992," *Advertising Age*, July 11, 1988; EC consumer numbers from Euromonitor Publications, Ltd., *Consumer Europe 1991* (London: 1991); EC disposable income from John Elkington, "Why It Pays to Be Green," *Financial Times*, October 14, 1989.

22. Das quoted in *Fortune*, March 26, 1990; Indian television from Elizabeth Bumiller, *May You Be the Mother of a Hundred Sons* (New York: Random House, 1990); Latin America from Sheldon Annis, "Giving Voice to the Poor," *Foreign Policy*, Fall 1991; world access to television is Worldwatch Institute estimate based on Euromonitor Publications Ltd., *European Marketing Data and Statistics 1987/88* (London: 1988), on United Nations Development Programme, *Human Development Report 1991* (New York: Oxford University Press, 1991), and on United Nations, *Statistical Yearbook 1987* (New York: 1990).

23. World television sets is Worldwatch Institute estimate based on United Nations, *Statistical Yearbook 1987* (New York: 1990); Bolivian Indians from Annis, "Giving Voice to the Poor"; Mongolian herders from "Tuning in the World," *Asiaweek*, October 25, 1991; Australian aborigines from Jim Beatson, "Dreamtime Beam," *South*, April 1990; Jerry Mander, *In the Absence of the Sacred* (San Francisco: Sierra Club Books, 1991); U.S. entertainment industry from John Huey, "America's Hottest Export: Pop Culture," *Fortune*, December 31, 1990.

24. Quote from Technology Management Group, press release, New Haven, Conn., September 3, 1991; Gilday quoted in Mander, *In the Absence of the Sacred*.

25. Declining time in conversation from Comstock, *Television in America*, from David P. Ross and Peter J. Usher, *From the Roots Up: Economic Development as if Community Mattered* (Croton-on-Hudson, N.Y.: The Bootstrap Press, 1986), from John S. Robinson, "How Americans Use Time," *The Futurist*, September/

October 1991, and from Tybor Scitovsky, *The Joyless Economy* (New York: Oxford University Press, 1976); TV fastest-growing time use from John P. Robinson, "What Do We Do With Our Time?" *American Demographics*, March 1987; 17th out of 22 from Bickley Townsend, "Time in Front of the Tube," *American Demographics*, May 1986.

26. Michael Maser, "Good Days, Bad Days," *Adbusters Quarterly* (Media Foundation, Vancouver), Fall/Winter 1991; teenagers, defined as aged 12–17, from John Schwartz, "Stalking the Youth Market," *Newsweek Special Issue*, June 1990; children from Comstock, *Television in America*; Center for Media and Values from Deborah Franklin, "Tuning the Kids In," *In Health*, December/January 1992.

27. Patrick Cooke, "TV or Not TV," *In Health*, December 1991/January 1992.

28. "American Excess," *Adbusters Quarterly* (Media Foundation, Vancouver), Summer 1990, and "The Media Movement Takes Root," *Adbusters Quarterly*, Fall/Winter 1991.

29. William Severini Kowinski, *The Malling of America* (New York: William Morrow & Co., Inc. 1985).

30. Total and annual number of malls from Michael J. McDermott, "Too Many Malls Are Chasing a Shrinking Supply of Shoppers," *Adweek's Marketing Week*, February 5, 1990; number of high schools from Schiller, *Culture, Inc.*; mall growth from Kara Swisher, "A Mall for America?" *Washington Post*, June 30, 1991; Potomac Mills from Marylou Tousignant and Brooke A. Masters, "The Buck Stops Here," *Washington Post*, September 8, 1991.

31. Swisher, "A Mall for America?"; retail sales from Donald L. Pendley, Director of Public Relations, International Council of Shopping Centers, New York, in "Malls Still Dominant" (letter), *American Demographics*, September 1990; France and Spain from Paula J. Silbey, "Spain Leads European Growth," *Shopping Centers Today*, March 1989.

32. Denver from U.S. Congress, Office of Technology Assessment, *Technology and the American Economic Transition: Choices for the Future* (Washington, D.C.: U.S. Government Printing Office, 1988).

33. Malls as entertainment centers from Dulcie Leimbach, "Acting Out Dreams of Athletic Prowess," *New York Times*, August 30, 1991, and from Roberta Brandes Gratz, "Malling the Northeast," *New York Times Magazine*, April 1, 1990; mall walkers from Mark J. Schoifet, "To AVIA, Mall Walking Is No Joke," *Shopping Centers Today*, January 1989, and from Bill Mintiens, Product Marketing Director for Walking, Avia, Portland, Oreg.,

private communication, July 3, 1990; Kowinski, *The Malling of America.*

34. Weekly shopping and church-going from Robert Fishman, "Megalopolis Unbound," *Wilson Quarterly,* Winter 1990; hours shopping and growth of shopping from Robinson, "How Americans Use Time"; teenagers from Kowinski, *The Malling of America.*

35. Teenage girls' favorite pastime from Laurence Shames, *The Hunger for More* (New York: Times Books, 1989); Tuff Stuff Shopping Basket from Karen Christensen, Great Barrington, Mass., private communication, February 25, 1992; Karen Christensen, "Don't Call me a Green Consumer," *Resurgence,* March/April 1991.

36. Spain from Silbey, "Spain Leads European Growth"; Stephen Baker and S. Lynne Walker, "The American Dream is Alive and Well—in Mexico," *Business Week,* September 30, 1991; "Development Sizzles in Puerto Rico," *Shopping Centers Today,* May 1991; number of superstores in Britain from Carl Gardner and Julie Sheppard, *Consuming Passion: The Rise of Retail Culture* (London: Unwin Hyman, 1990); floor space in Britain from "No Frills, Please," *Economist,* July 20, 1991; Paula J. Silbey, "Italian Centers Expected to Triple in Number Soon," *Shopping Centers Today,* May 1989; "France: Aging but Dynamic," *Market: Europe* (Ithaca, N.Y.), September 1990.

37. Japan from Arthur Getz, "Small Town Economics, West and East," letter to Peter Martin, Institute of Current World Affairs, Hanover, N.H., December 26, 1989; Large-Scale Retail Store Law from "Toy Joy," *Economist,* January 4, 1992.

38. Fish wrap from Yorimoto Katsumi, "Tokyo's Serious Waste Problem," *Japan Quarterly,* July/September 1990; Toys "R" Us from Clayton Jones, "A Cool Forecast for Japan in 1991," *Christian Science Monitor,* January 3, 1991; new store and mall construction from Diane Durston, "Small is Beautiful," *Far Eastern Economic Review,* March 28, 1991; malls per month from "Harper's Index," *Harper's,* May 1991; malls by 2000 and their contents from Yumiko Ono, "Japan Becomes Land of the Rising Mall," *Wall Street Journal,* February 11, 1991.

39. Japan from Durston, "Small is Beautiful"; Massachusetts from Barbara Flanagan, "A Cape Cod Mall is Disappeared," *New York Times,* March 14, 1991.

40. Timothy Harper, "British Sunday Law Intact—for Now," *Shopping Centers Today,* May 1989; green belts from Timothy Harper, "Rulings Slow U.K. Mall Development," *Shopping Centers Today,* May 1989.

CHAPTER 10. A Culture of Permanence

1. Basic value of sustainable society from World Commission on Environment and Development, *Our Common Future* (New York: Oxford University Press, 1987).
2. Scott Willis, *The San Jose Mercury News*, San Jose, Calif., 1989.
3. Paul Wachtel, *The Poverty of Affluence* (Philadelphia: New Society Publishers, 1989). The sole exception to this generalization is travel, which many people find richly rewarding but which is environmentally destructive when done by airplane or car.
4. Aristotle, *Nicomachean Ethics* 1109b23.
5. Sidney Quarrier, geologist, Connecticut Geological & Natural History Survey, Hartford, Conn., private communication, February 25, 1992.
6. EarthWorks Group, Berkeley, Calif., private communication, February 25, 1992.
7. Duane Elgin, *Voluntary Simplicity* (New York: William Morrow and Company, 1981); United Kingdom and Germany from Pierre Pradervand, independent researcher, Geneva, Switzerland, private communication, July 14, 1990, and from Groupe de Beaulieu, *Construire L'Esperance* (Lausanne: Editions de l'Aire, 1990); India from Mark Shepard, *Gandhi Today: A Report on Mahatma Gandhi's Successors* (Arcata, Calif.: Simple Productions, 1987); Netherlands and Norway from Elgin, *Voluntary Simplicity*.
8. Rewards of simplicity from Wendell Berry, *The Gift of Good Land* (San Francisco: North Point Press, 1981), from "What Is Enough?" *In Context* (Bainbridge Island, Wash.), Summer 1990, and from Katy Butler, "Paté Poverty: Downwardly Mobile Baby Boomers Lust After Luxury," *Utne Reader*, September/October 1989; Karen Christensen, "With the Earth in Mind: the Personal to the Political," in Sara Parkins, ed., *Green Light on Europe* (London: Heretic Books, 1991).
9. New Road Map Foundation from Vicki Robin, president, New Road Map Foundation, Seattle, Wash., various private communications, 1990-92, and from Vicki Robin, "How Much Is Enough?" *In Context* (Bainbridge Island, Wash.), Summer 1990; number of participants from Nick Ravo, "For the 90's, Lavish Amounts of Stinginess," *New York Times*, January 15, 1992.
10. Frank Levering and Wanda Urbanska, *Simple Living: One Couple's Search for a Better Life* (New York: Viking Penguin, 1992).
11. Joanne Forman, Ranchos de Taos, N.M., private communication, August 28, 1991, edited slightly to shorten.

12. David Shi, *The Simple Life: Plain Living and High Thinking in American Culture* (New York: Oxford University Press, 1985).
13. Cuba from Lee Hockstader, "Communists Press Forth—By Oxcart," *Washington Post*, September 12, 1991.
14. Toynbee quoted in Wachtel, *Poverty of Affluence*.
15. Thales from Goldian VandenBroeck, ed., *Less Is More: The Art of Voluntary Poverty* (New York: Harper & Row, 1978).
16. Bible and Saints Augustine and Francis from VandenBroek, *Less is More*; Thomas Aquinas from Benjamin Kline Hunnicutt, *Work Without End: Abandoning Shorter Hours for the Right to Work* (Philadelphia: Temple U. Press, 1988); monks and merchants from Herman E. Daly and John B. Cobb, Jr., *For the Common Good: Redirecting the Economy Toward Community, the Environment, and a Sustainable Future* (Boston: Beacon Press, 1989).
17. Freya Littledale, adapter, *The Magic Fish* (New York: Scholastic, Inc., 1966); King Midas from Edith Hamilton, *Mythology* (Boston: Little Brown and Co., 1942).
18. Franklin quoted in Herb Goldberg and Robert T. Lewis, *Money Madness: The Psychology of Saving, Spending, Loving and Hating Money* (New York: William Morrow & Co., 1978); Patten quoted in Henry Allen, "Bye-Bye America's Pie," *Washington Post*, February 11, 1992.
19. Peter Weber, "Last Gasp for U.S. Smokers," *World Watch*, November/December 1990.
20. Michael A. O'Connell and Michael Sutton, "The Effects of Trade Moratoria on International Commerce in African Elephant Ivory: A Preliminary Report," World Wildlife Fund and The Conservation Foundation, Washington, D.C., June 1990.
21. Robert Bellah, *The Broken Covenant* (New York: Seabury Press, 1975).
22. Car travel is 1988 vehicle-kilometers per capita in West Germany based on International Roads Federation, *World Road Statistics 1984-88* (Washington, D.C.: 1989); Dutch household packaging waste is Worldwatch Institute estimate based on J.M. Joosten et al., *Informative Document: Packaging Waste* (Bilthoven, Netherlands: National Institute of Public Health and Environmental Protection, 1989); mail from Blayne Cutler, "Meet Jane Doe," *American Demographics*, June 1989; land developed from Jim Riggle, Director of Operations, American Farmland Trust, Washington, D.C., private communication, October 17, 1990.
23. Polls in the United States found 71 percent supporting the environment versus economic growth, while in the European Community the share was 55 percent, according to Organisation for

Economic Co-operation and Development, *State of the Environment, 1991* (Paris: 1991); Richard A. Easterlin and Eileen M. Crimmins, "Private Materialism, Personal Self-Fulfillment, Family Life, and Public Interest: The Nature, Effects, and Causes of Recent Changes in the Values of American Youth," *Public Opinion Quarterly*, Vol. 55, 1991; Wacker quoted in Allen, "Bye-Bye America's Pie."

24. Fabric stores from Janice Castro, "Hunkering Down," *Time*, July 23, 1990; other signs of simplifying from Amy Saltzman, "The New Meaning of Success," *U.S. News & World Report*, September 17, 1990, from Joseph T. Plummer, "Changing Values," *The Futurist*, January/February 1989, and from Ronald Henkoff, "Is Greed Dead?" *Fortune*, August 14, 1989; *Tightwad Gazette* (Leeds, Maine), various editions; subscribers from Ravo, "For the 90's, Lavish Amounts of Stinginess."

25. Henry David Thoreau, *Walden* (1854; reprint, Boston: Houghton Mifflin, 1957).

# Index

acid rain, 51, 82
Action for Children's Television, 123
advertising
  bans, 123
  to children, 120–21, 123, 125, 128
  and consumerism, 36, 119, 120, 122
  ecological dangers of, 122
  environmental claims, 96–97,
    124–25
  expenditures, 96, 121
  fashion, 96
  grassroots challenges to, 128–29
  industry growth, 36, 120
  information in, 118–19, 123, 129
  mail, 122, 148
  in public spaces, 129–30
  reforms, 123–25, 135
  saturation, 121–22
  on television, 123, 128–29
  tobacco and alcohol, 123, 125
  volume of, 118
  women as targets of, 119–20
  see also mass marketing
Africa, television in, 22, 126
agriculture
  energy use for, 68, 69
  and environmental degradation, 56,
    68, 75
  reforms, 69
  slash-and-burn, 23, 51, 75
  subsidies, 110
air conditioning, 32, 51, 84
air pollution
  fuel use and, 51, 79, 82
  industries ranking highest, 52
  transport mode and, 80, 85
air travel, 29, 30, 31, 85
  energy costs of, 79, 85
  environmental costs of, 85
  jet set, 84–85
  pollution taxes on, 88
  reforms, 87–88
Allied Stores Corporation, 119
Alperson, Myra, 87
aluminum
  beverage cans, 70
  consumption, 29, 31, 50, 51
  production costs, 56, 70
  subsidies, 110
  waste disposal, 70
Amazon, 58, 97
American Academy of Pediatrics, 123

appliances
  household ownership, 32
  planned obsolescence and
    disposability, 94–95
  recycling of, 99
aquaculture, 75–76
Argyle, Michael, 39, 42
Aristotle, 37, 138
Association of Forest Service Employees
  for Environmental Ethics, 98–99
Australia, 80, 123
Australian Consumers' Association, 123
automobiles
  and air pollution, 35, 80, 138
  and community structure, 83–84, 108,
    148
  distances traveled in, 80–81, 83–84,
    148
  environmental impacts of, 82–83,
    138
  fuel efficiency, 59, 82
  and land use, 83
  leisure and, 47
  marketing of, 81–82
  materials used in, 83
  ownership, 29, 30, 31, 33, 35, 36, 47,
    80–81
  recycling of, 99
  replacement with other transport
    modes, 109
  as a status symbol, 82, 138
  subsidies, 110
  and traffic fatalities, 82
Avia, 131

Bangladesh, 57–58
Barbie dolls, 122
Barthes, Roland, 81
Bellah, Robert, 147
Berry, Wendell, 89, 90, 95
beverages
  containers, 70, 71–72, 73
  soft drinks, 31, 31, 71
  transport of, 72
  see also diet; food and drink
bicycles
  benefits of, 59, 79, 85, 109
  promotion of, 80, 85, 86, 88
  shipments of, to developing countries,
    87
  use in Cuba, 142
Borneo, 56
Boston Consulting Group, 120
Botswana, 75, 97
Braun company, 99
Brazil
  auto ownership, 81
  environmental degradation, 55–56, 97
  export industries, 55–56

Briars, David, 122–23
buses, 59, 79, 80, 85, 86

Canada, 99, 122
carbon emissions, 49, 60, 82, 85, 91, 111
Carleton College, 76
cars, see automobiles
cement
  consumption, 29, 31, 50, 90–92
  environmental costs of production, 91
Center for Media and Values, 128
Center for the Study of Commercialism,
  125
China
  packaging industry, 93
  transport modes, 79, 80
chlorofluorocarbons, 51
Christensen, Karen, 132, 140
cigarettes, 31, 145
climate, stabilization, 60
clothes dryers, 32, 60
clothing
  Barbie dolls as a medium for, 122
  children's concerns about, 120
  ecological damage by fashion market,
    96
  leisure wear as replacement for leisure,
    47
  marketing of, 95–96, 120, 122
coastal ecosystems, damage to, 75–76
Coca-Cola Company, 30–31, 71, 118
cocaine industry, 58
commodity booms, 57–58
community structure
  automobiles and, 83–84, 86, 108
  neighborhoods, 46, 74, 130–31
  shopping malls and, 46, 74, 130–31,
    134
Connett, Ellen and Paul, 100
consumer class
  auto ownership, 81
  birth of, 21–22, 29
  diet, 27, 28, 58, 67–68, 69–70, 72
  earnings, 27–28
  energy use, 49, 52, 92
  environmental harm by, 23, 51–52, 54
  geographic distribution, 28, 30–31, 35
  greenhouse gas emissions, 49, 54
  growth of, 30–31
  guidelines for informing, 138–39
  health of, 68
  housing, 28
  life-style, 28
  materials consumption, 27, 29, 54, 92
  television role, 128
  transformation of, 24–25, 100–01,
    137–39, 145–50
  travel/transport, 27, 28, 79, 80–81, 84
consumer cooperatives, 76–77

consumer durables, 94, 95, 109
consumer society, see consumer class
consumerism
  advertising and, 117, 120–22, 129
  in children, 121
  and commodity booms, 57–58
  and community changes, 46
  cultural and folk teachings on, 144–45
  definition, 49
  extravagances of the eighties, 33
  green, 124–25
  growth of, 30–36
  and happiness, 34, 38, 40, 61, 147
  and household changes, 45–46
  international effects of, 54–56
  opposition to, 135, 138–39, 143–145
  and pace of life, 46–47
  promotion of, 117, 141–42
  roots of, 142–43, 145–46
  and social relations, 43
  television and, 35–36, 125–26
consumption, see materials consumption
cost of living index, 30
Crimmins, Eileen, 43–44
Cuba, 39, 142

Dacyczyn, Amy, 149
Daly, Herman, 59
Das, Gurcharan, 126
Debonis, Jeff, 98
deforestation, 23, 51, 56, 66, 75
Denmark, ban on disposable containers, 72–73
developing countries
  advertising industry growth in, 120
  auto use, 80
  effect of decline in industrial country-consumption, 106, 111
  environmental degradation in, 55, 56
  exports of natural resources, 55–56, 111
  resource consumption, 50–51
  waterborne diseases, 65
  see also individual countries
diet
  fish consumers, 50
  grain consumers, 50, 65, 90
  and health, 68
  high-fat, 56, 67–68, 149
  junk food, 69, 74, 123, 149
  meat consumers, 29, 31, 50, 67–68, 75
  nutrition guidelines, 67–68, 69
  reforms, 68–69
  see also Food and drink
disposable products, 44
  ban on, 72–73
  batteries, 94
  cameras, 93–94
  containers, 31, 72

diapers, 45, 93
pens, 94
picnic ware, 94
pricing of, 110
razors, 94
spray paint cans, 94
videocassettes, 94
Dominguez, Joe, 140
Dourojeanni, Marc, 58
drinking water
  access to, 65
  as a beverage, 66
  bottled, 71, 73–74
  transport of, 73–74, 77
Duany, Andres, 134
Dutko, Nancy, 87

Earth Day 1990, 19
Earthsave, 69
Eastman Kodak, 115
economic policies
  consumption as a goal of, 21, 29–30, 33, 105
  and poverty alleviation, 111–12
economy
  burden on ecological systems, 59
  low-consumption, 106–08
  of permanence, 112–13, 136–50
Eggverts International, 118
Egli, Robert, 85
Ekins, Paul, 34
elderly people, prosperity and happiness, 42–43
Elgin, Duane, 139
employment
  bans on overtime, 114–15
  consumption and, 106, 108–09, 116
  flexible arrangements in, 115
  and happiness, 42, 114
  labor intensity and environmental impact, 109
  part-time, 114, 115
  tax reforms and, 111, 112
  transition to low consumption, 109, 111
  voluntary work-time reduction programs, 115
  workweek, 24, 47–48, 108–09, 112–15
endangered species, 57
energy crises, 31
energy use
  for agriculture, 68
  for cement production, 91
  computation, 20
  for food processing, packaging, and distribution, 69
  for fuel production, 82–83
  by home appliances, 32
  by incinerators, 99–100

energy use *(cont'd)*
    industrial vs. developing countries, 50,
        51
    for packaging, 69, 93
    for paper production, 122
    per capita, by country, 53
    pollution from, 49, 52, 56
    for resource production, 56, 90
    transport mode and, 79, 85
    trends, 29, 31, 52
    see also fossil fuels
environmental degradation, 136–37
    advertising and, 122–23
    agriculture and, 56,.68, 75
    educating consumers about, 138
    energy use and, 49–51, 82–83
    export industries in developing
        countries and, 55–56
    food-related, 66, 68, 69, 75–76
    industry rankings for, 52
    international effects of consumerism,
        54–55
    livestock production and, 56, 75
    materials extraction and processing
        and, 89–91, 92–93
    from paper making, 122–23
    poverty and, 23–24, 51, 65
    pricing of resources and, 110, 112
    public opinion on, 148
    subsidies and, 24, 55
    technology and, 59–60
    trade and, 56–58, 75
    transportation and, 35, 59–60, 79, 80,
        82–83, 85
Esprit, 96
ethical issues, 136–37
Europe (Eastern and Central)
    advertising industry growth in, 120
    auto ownership, 81
    consumerist class, 35
Europe (Western)
    auto use and ownership, 31, 80
    carbon emissions tax, 111
    diet, 31, 70
    disposable containers, 72
    farm policy reforms, 69
    "green labeling" program, 124
    imports from developing countries,
        56–57
    materials consumption, 31, 32
    shopping restrictions, 135
    television standards, 123, 126
    workweek, 113, 116
    see also individual countries
Everything Goes Furniture, 100

families and households, 43–44
    child care, 45
    gardening, 45–46

housework, 44–45, 70
    time off from work for, 115
    transformation in economics of, 44–46
fashion, see clothing
fast food, 31, 36, 45
Finland, 73
food and drink
    advertising, 123
    delicacies, 58, 75–76
    energy use related to, 69, 70
    environmental damage related to, 66,
        68, 69
    farmers' markets, 76
    frozen, 31, 69–70
    garden production, 45–46
    global supply lines, 75–76
    local, unprocessed, 45–46, 76, 110–11
    reforms related to, 76–77, 109, 110–11
    processing, 69
    packaged, processed items, 29, 31, 44
    packaging, 31, 45, 67, 69, 70–71
    retailing, structural changes in, 74–75,
        110–11
    shrimp and shellfish production, 75–76
    transport, 45, 69, 73, 74–75, 77
    see also beverages; diet
forestry reforms, 98–99
Forman, Joanne, 141
fossil fuels
    carbon emissions, 82, 85
    consumer class use of, 52, 92
    and environmental degradation, 49,
        51, 82–83
    potential for reducing consumption, 60
    prices, 110
    see also energy use
France
    energy subsidies, 110
    environmental advertising code, 124
    mall development, 133
    materials consumption, 31
    workweek, 113
Franklin, Benjamin, 145
Friedman, Meryl, 121–22
Friends of the Earth-U.K., 87
Frugal Zealot, 149
fur coats, 33, 57

gardening, 45–46, 114
Gardner, Carl, 46
Germany (East), mass marketing in, 31
Germany (West)
    materials consumption, 31
    paper consumption, 93
    reuse and recycling of packaging, 73,
        99
    satisfaction with life, 39
    trade restrictions, 135
    travel/transport, 148

workweek, 113
Gilday, Cindy, 127
global warming, 85
gold mining, 97
Goldemberg, José, 60
Gomberg, Tooker, 88
Great Depression, 30, 106, 114
greenhouse gases, 49, 66, 85
Grenier, Dianne, 129

happiness
    consumerism and, 34, 37–38, 61, 147
    determinants of, 41–42, 48, 113
    leisure and, 25, 41
    income and, 39–40
    wealth and, 23, 38–39, 145
hazardous wastes, 51, 58, 96
Hendrix College, 76
Hideo, Takayama, 120
Himalayan deer, 57
H.J. Heinz, 126
Hocker, Phil, 98
homeless people, 22
households, see families and households
housing, design changes, 45
hunger, 66
Hunkin, Tim, 94
hunting, for trade, 57–58

illegal drug production, 57, 58
Illich, Ivan, 92, 117
income
    and consumption of ecologically
        damaging products, 52
    and happiness, 39–40, 42
    world average, 22
India
    advertising industry growth in, 120
    auto ownership in, 82
    consumerism in, 35–36, 82
    cultivation of marginal lands, 23
    satisfaction with life, 39
    television in, 126–27
    trade and environmental degradation,
        57–58
    transport modes, 79–80
Indonesia
    pace of life, 47
    shopping malls, 36
    trade and environmental degradation,
        57–58, 76
industrial countries
    consumption as a measure of success,
        22
    imports from developing countries,
        56–57
    resource consumption, 50–51, 53
    solid waste, 93
    see also individual countries

Institute of Statistical Mathematics, 34
Intergovernmental Panel on Climate
    Change, 60
International Advertising Association,
    126
irrigation, 68, 96, 110
Italy, 47, 133
ivory trade, 146–47

Japan
    agricultural imports, 56
    appliance ownership in households, 32
    car ownership, 31, 47, 80–81, 82
    commerce patterns, 133–34
    consumerism, growth in, 30, 31–32,
        33, 82
    Council of Shopping Centers, 134
    death from overwork (karoshi), 116
    diet, 31, 70
    disposable containers, 72
    Disneyland (near Tokyo), 30
    disposables, 93–94
    energy use, 31
    "green labeling" program, 124
    imports from developing countries,
        56–57, 76
    Large-Scale Retail Store Law, 133
    leisure boom (reja bumu), 47
    marketing to children in, 120
    pace of life, 47
    packaging, 134
    paved roads, 83
    pedestrian heavens (hokoosha
        tengoku), 133
    philosophy of life, 34
    resource consumption, 31
    satisfaction with life, 39
    Seikatsu Club Consumers'
        Cooperatives, 77
    shopping mall development, 133–34
    subsidies, 110
    success measures, 22
    trade surplus, 33
    travel/transport system, 31, 80, 84
    workweek, 113, 116

Katsumi, Yorimoto, 33
Keng, Chiam Heng, 121
Keough, Donald R., 71
Kim, Peter, 119
Kowinski, William, 131

L.A. Gear, 96
land use
    planning, 148
    transport mode and, 83
    undervaluation of resources and, 110
landfills, 70
Lapham, Lewis, 38

Larson, Eric, 53
Latin America, television in, 127
Lebow, Victor, 21–22
leisure
    happiness and, 25, 41, 42, 48, 114
    and shopping, 128
    and television viewing, 114, 125,
        127–28, 132
    uses of, 114, 137–38
    value of, 47
    wealth accumulation and, 23
    wear, 47
Levering, Frank, 140–41
Levine, Robert, 47
life-style
    reforms, 68–69
    U.S., 22
    voluntary simplicity, 139–42
Lindquist, John, 120
livestock production
    developing country role in, 56
    energy use for, 69
    environmental effects, 56, 75, 96
    grain for feed, 57, 68
    grazing on public lands, 69
    and farm policy reforms, 69
logging, 110, 122
luxury goods, 22, 97

Malaysia, 56, 75, 112, 121
Mander, Jerry, 127
mangroves, 75–76
Maser, Michael, 128
mass marketing
    of automobiles, 81–82
    of beverages, 71
    to children, 120–21, 123
    fashion industry, 96
    techniques, 31, 117, 118, 122, 124,
        128
    to teenagers, 96
    see also advertising
materialism, 89, 121, 148
materials consumption
    addictiveness of, 40–41
    classes of consumers, see consumer
        class; middle-income class; poor
        people
    economic effects of decline in, 106–08,
        116
    as economic policy goal, 21, 29–30,
        105–06
    and employment, 106, 108, 109–10,
        116
    by individuals, 19–20
    inequities in, 22–23
    as measure of success, 22, 34
    as patriotic duty, 30
    proxies for, 90

reforms in, 25, 97–98, 145–50
religious teachings on, 143–44
and social values, 22
sustainable levels, 24–25
transition to low levels, 109–10,
    146–50
trends, 29, 53–54
see also consumerism; resource
    consumption
Mattel, 121–22, 132
McCrory, Colleen, 122
McDonald's restaurants, 31, 124–25
meat, see diet; food and drink; livestock
    production
Media Foundation, 129
men
    housework by, 44–45, 70
    work-time, 115–16
Mexico
    car ownership, 36
    consumerism in, 36
    mall development in, 132
    success measures, 22
microwave ovens, 32, 133
middle-income class
    carbon emissions from energy use,
        49
    diet, 27, 66
    earnings, 27, 66, 140
    energy use, 52
    environmental degradation caused by,
        51, 66–67
    geographic distribution, 27
    health of, 66
    housing, 27
    materials consumption, 27, 29, 91–92
    population size, 27
    transport modes, 27, 79–80, 85–86
mining
    and environmental degradation, 97
    reforms, 98
money, see income; wealth

National Association of Dumpster Divers
    and Urban Miners, 100
National Association of Railroad
    Passengers, 77
National Opinion Research Center,
    38–39
National Prosperity Bureau, 30
Natural Resources Defense Council, 69
neighborhoods, 46, 74, 130–31
Netherlands
    agricultural imports, 56
    environmental advertising code, 124
    reuse and recycling of packaging, 73
Neves, Ricardo, 88
New Road Map Foundation, 140
New Ways to Work, 115

newly industrializing countries, car
  ownership, 81
Nicaragua, 72
nitrogen emissions, 51, 52, 85
noise pollution, 82
North America
  auto ownership and use, 80
  disposable containers, 72
  forestry reforms, 98–99
  "green labeling" program, 124
  imports from developing countries,
    56–57
  paved roads, 83
  see also individual countries

oil drilling and refining, 82–83
Olmstead, Barney, 115
ozone
  stratospheric layer depletion, 32, 51,
    84, 85
  tropospheric pollution, 85

pace of life, 46–47, 78
packaging
  amount generated by individuals, 20
  benefits of, 69, 72
  consumer pressures to reduce, 124–25
  cosmetic, 70
  disposable containers, 31, 72
  elimination of, 76
  energy consumed in, 69, 93
  environmental costs of, 110
  food and drink, 45, 69, 70, 71, 93,
    124–25
  paper, 20, 70, 93, 134
  plastic, 93, 134
  and pricing of products, 93, 110
  refillable containers, 71–73
  reuse and recycling, 73, 99
  "Save Our Bottles" campaign, 73
  single-use containers, 71
  styrofoam packing, 94, 134
  waste generated by, 93
  "Wrapping Is a Rip Off" campaign, 72
Panama, 39, 76
paper
  for advertising, 122
  consumption, 31, 50, 90–92, 93
  environmental impacts of production,
    91, 110
  packaging, 20, 70, 93
Parikh, Jyoti, 51–52
Patten, Simon Nelson, 145
PepsiCo, Ltd., 71
Perrier, 74
pesticides, 58, 68, 75, 96
petrochemical industry, 96
Philippines
  Baatan export processing zone, 55

cultivation of marginal lands, 23
  environmental degradation in, 55, 76
  satisfaction with life, 39
plastics
  appliance parts, 94
  consumption, 29, 30, 83, 93
  packaging, 93, 134
  production, 83
Plater-Zyberk, Elizabeth, 134
pollution
  taxes, 88, 111
  toxic emissions, 83, 90, 94, 110,
    122–23
  see also air pollution; individual
    pollutants
poor people
  carbon emissions from energy use, 49
  diet, 26, 27, 65–66
  drinking water, 65
  earnings, 26, 27
  energy use, 52
  environmental degradation by, 66, 90,
    137
  geographic distribution, 26, 66
  health of, 65
  housing, 26
  materials consumption, 26–27, 29, 90
  population size, 26
  television viewing, 127
  travel/transport, 26, 27, 79
  see also poverty
population
  size and growth, 59
  stabilization, 60
poverty
  alleviation of, 111–12
  and environmental degradation,
    23–24, 51, 65
Procter & Gamble, 124–25, 126
public transit, 84, 87, 108
Public Voice on Food and Health Policy,
  69
Puckett, B. Earl, 119

Quarrier, Sidney, 19–21, 138

rail transport
  employment, 109
  environmental costs of, 59, 80
  impediments to, 77, 84, 85
  resource consumption, 109
  use in developing countries, 79–80
rain forests, deforestation, 23, 56, 75
Ramm, Ulrich, 35
Rams, Dieter, 99
rangelands, overgrazing, 23
rapidly industrializing nations,
  consumerism in, 36
refrigerators, 32

Reilly, Anthony J.F., 126
religion, and consumerism, 143–44
Replogle, Michael, 87
resources
    consumption, see material
        consumption
    energy use in production, 56, 90
    extraction and processing, 89–90, 92,
        97
    physical flows in economy of
        permanence, 108
    precious metals and gems, 97
    undervaluation of, 95, 110, 112
reuse and recycling
    of appliances, 95
    employment in, 109
    furniture, 100
    hand tools for developing countries,
        100
    incineration contrasted with, 99–100,
        109
    by middle-income class, 92, 97–98
    "Save Our Bottles" campaign, 73
rich people
    billionaires, 22
    carbon emissions from energy use,
        49–50
    earnings, 28–29
    jet setters, 84–85
    materials consumption, 97
    millionaires, 22, 41–42
roads, 46, 83
Roberts, Glyn, 100
Russia, 110
Rybczynski, Witold, 47–48

Saint Olaf College, 76
satisfaction, see happiness
schools, advertising-free zones, 125
Schor, Juliet, 113, 114
Schumacher, E.F., 47
Scitovsky, Tibor, 40, 42
sea turtle destruction, 57
Seabrook, Jeremy, 42–43
Services Employees International, 115
Shephard, Julie, 46
Shi, David, 142
shoes, marketing of, 96, 122, 131
shopping
    changes in patterns of, 148–49
    convenience stores, 74
    as a cultural activity, 131–32
    as entertainment, 131
    food retailing, 74
    hypermarkets, 74
    leisure time used for, 128
    Mall of America, 130
    malls, 36, 46, 129–31, 133–34
    opposition to shopping centers, 134

Potomac Mills mall, 130
    replacement of malls with towns, 134
    Sunday, restrictions on trade, 135
    supermarkets, 74
Sinclair, Louise, 99
Singapore, mass marketing in, 31
Skinner, Mark, 87
social relations
    happiness and, 23, 41, 42, 48
    mutual dependence, 43
soil degradation, 56, 66, 68, 75
solid waste
    composition of, 70, 93
    sorting valuables out of trash, 100
South Korea
    advertising industry growth in, 120
    auto ownership, 81
    consumerism in, 36
species extinctions, 51, 57
standard of living, 41, 59–60
steel
    consumption, 29, 31, 50, 83, 90–92
    production costs, 56
Stumpf, William, 113
subsidies
    agricultural, 69
    and environmental degradation, 24,
        55, 98
    fuel, 77
    for grazing on public lands, 69
    and resource consumption, 108, 110,
        112
sulfur oxides, 51, 52, 122
Sweden, transportation reforms, 86,
    87–88

taxes
    employment and, 111
    fuel subsidies, 77
    pollution, 88, 111
    reforms, 87–88, 112
    and resource consumption, 108, 110
    transport, 87–88
technology
    environmental performance of, 59, 60
    and food and beverage systems
        reforms, 77
    and materials use, 98
television
    advertising, 123, 128–29
    and conversation, 128
    and cultural homogenization, 127–28
    depictions of success, 22
    deregulation in Europe, 126
    disposal of sets, 95
    as educational tool, 126
    grassroots challenges to, 128–29
    and growth of consumerism, 35–36,
        125–26

leisure time and viewing time, 114,
  125, 127–28, 132
programming standards for, 123
transition to nonconsuming ends, 129
Tetra Pak, 72
Texaco, 124
Thoreau, Henry David, 150
timber consumption, 29, 50
time-use surveys, 83–84
tires, recycling, 95
Tolstoy, Leo, 37
Tools for Self Reliance, 100
Töpfer, Klaus, 99
toys, 122, 132
Toys "R" Us, Inc., 134
toxic emissions, 83, 90, 94, 110, 122–23
trade
  and environmental degradation, 56–58
  reforms, 112, 133–34
  U.S. pressures on Japan, 133–34
transport/travel
  distances, 83–84, 148
  energy use in, 45, 69, 73
  environmental costs of, 35, 59–60, 79,
    80, 82–83, 85
  environmentally sound, 85–86
  of foods, 45, 69, 73, 77
  leisure and, 47
  in low-consumption economy, 108
  patterns of economic classes, 78–81
  reforms, 77, 86–88, 109
  see also individual modes
trucks/trucking, 77, 82

United Kingdom
  auto subsidies, 110
  disposables, 93
  energy use in packaging, 93
  gardening, 46
  green belts, 135
  materials consumption, 31
  pace of life, 47
  shopping centers, 133
  trade restrictions, 135
  Vegetarian Society of, 69
  Women's Environment Network, 72
  women's roles, 44–45
United States
  advertising in, 120–22, 124
  air travel, 30
  antiurban growth activists, 134
  appliance ownership, 32
  automobile ownership, 30, 33
  beef production inputs, 68
  beverage consumption, 71
  children's market in, 121
  Council of Economic Advisers, 30
  disposables, 94
  extravagances of the eighties, 33

farm policy reforms, 69
food imports, 76
forestry reforms, 98–99, 110
General Mining Act of 1872, 98
life-style, 22
mineral resource consumption, 38
mining on federal lands, 98, 110
pace of life, 47
parenthood, 43–44
personal debt, 33
philosophy of life, 34, 43–44
plastic consumption, 30, 93
poverty line, 22
satisfaction with life, 38–39
shopping malls, 130
social relations, 43
social values, 22
solid waste, 70
television programming exports, 127
travel, 30
women's roles, 44–45
worker productivity, 113
workweek, 113
Urban Ore, 100
urban sprawl, 84, 86, 131
Urbanska, Wanda, 140–41

Veblen, Thorstein, 40
Valéry, Paul, 78
Vegetarian Society of the U.K., 69
Ventrudo, Kevin, 96
video cassette recorders, 32
volatile organic compounds, 52
voluntary simplicity, 139–42

Wacker, Watts, 148
washing machines, 32
Washington State,
  recycling-or-incinerate struggle, 100
waste disposal
  fees, 99
  incineration, 99–100, 109
  in landfills, 70, 99, 109
water
  consumption, industrial vs. developing
    countries, 50, 51
  depletion, 68
  for paper production, 122
  pollution, 68
  use for meat production, 68
  see also drinking water
wealth
  distribution of, 22
  and happiness, 23, 38, 41–42, 145
  importance in U.S., 34–35, 40
  and self-worth, 40
Wilde, Oscar, 95
Wilder, Laura Ingalls, 97–98
wildlife trade, 57

W.K. Kellogg Company, 114
women
    household role, 44–45
    shopping as a role for, 132
Women's Environment Network, 72

Women's Legal Defense Fund, 115
workweek, 24, 47–48, 108–09, 112–13

Yankelovich Clancy Shulman, 148–49
Yugoslavia, 39